William C. Tyler

CRITICAL THINKING

A PRIMER

Old Stone Press

Critical Thinking – A Primer
By William C. Tyler

Published by Old Stone Press
an imprint of J. H. Clark & Associates, Inc.
Louisville, Kentucky 40207 USA
www.oldstonepress.com

© 2018, William C. Tyler

All rights reserved.

This Advance Reader Copy is an uncorrected proof whose price and publication date is subject to change. Reviewers, please direct spelling errors, grammar errors, typos or format errors and [heaven forbid] any content errors or any general comments about the book to the author, William C. Tyler at wctyler4@gmail.com or as a last resort to the publisher Old Stone Press, attention J. H. Clark at john@oldstonepress.com.

This book may not be reproduced in whole or in part without written permission from the publisher, Old Stone Press, or from the author, William C. Tyler, except by a reviewer who may quote brief passages in a review; nor any part of this book be reproduced, stored in a retrieval system, or transmitted in any form or by any means, electronic, mechanical photocopying, recording or other, without written permission from the publisher or author.

For information about special discounts for bulk purchases or autographed copies of this book, please contact J. H. Clark, Old Stone Press at john@oldstonepress.com or the author William C. Tyler at wctyler4@gmail.com

---

This is not a work of fiction. It is a "memoir" and a labor of love by William C. Tyler for his family, friends and many generations of Tylers and their friends and families to come. Names, characters, businesses, places, events and incidents for the most part do not fall into the category of "fake news," which means they could be alternate facts meant to be true, but best remembered in the imagination of the author at the time of this writing. The author swears they are true and means every word of it. A true "Tyler" teaching moment. Any resemblance to actual persons, living or dead, or actual events is not purely coincidental. The publisher is not liable for any of the content in this "memoir."

Critical Thinking - A Primer
By William C. Tyler
ISBN: 978-1-938462-33-7
Library of Congress Control Number: 2018942481

Published in the United States

DEDICATION & APPRECIATION

I *would like* to dedicate the book to my parents Claudia and Sam Tyler, brother Gwthmey's first wife, Nina Tyler, and nephew Welby Tyler.

I also want to thank my three "partners in crime," brothers Gwathmey, Robin and Terry. My wife Beth, daughter Meg and her husband Jeff Foster, son Will and his wife Hayley, for their encouragement, patience, and technical assistance.

Finally, I want to thank Mitzi Kintz for her extensive first edit and Anne Warner for declining to edit. Yes, this book was a labor of love.

CONTENTS

Prologue 9

In the Beginning. 11

Anchorage 13

Maine 17

Birthdays 20

2nd Grade Brought Polio 21

What is It? 24

Treatment Begins 27

Nanny 29

Easter Debut 31

Cape May, New Jersey and The Chalfonte Hotel 33

Louisville History 37

The Tyler Estate 39

The Train 41

First Responders 44

3rd Grade Begins 46

Thanksgiving 47

Cave Hill Cemetery 48

Christmas 1955 50

Colgan's Christmas Dinner 53

Viola P. Jones 55

Gwathmey and Robin 60

Louisville Country Club 61
St. Luke's Fair and Horse Show 63
The Kentucky Derby 66
13 Acres 69
The Athenaeum Literary Association 74
Cape May Annuals 79
Richard M. Nixon Lights My Republican Flame 88
Humor 101
A Strategic Critical Thinking Example 104
Go Carts 108
Anchorage Telephone and Telegraph 110
More Tyler Brother Traditions 112
Sophomore Year at Waggener 122
W&L Awakening 130
W&L Junior Year 135
Emory Business School 146
Working For CSRI 150
The Masters in Augusta 157
Beth and I Get Married 159
Working for CBRE 162
Tyler Yates Financial Group 167
Cumstoun and the Maitland Family in Scotland 168
"May Day, May Day! Dog House One? This is Dog House Two!" 171
Only the Pizza Man Gets Paid 173
The Tyler Dynasty Grows 175
Holliday Fenoglio and Tyler 179

Back to the New and Improved CBRE 181
Meg Marries Jeff Foster 184
Will and Hayley Get Married 188
Life's Unexpected Pleasures 190

PROLOGUE

The first discussion of critical thinking dates back 2400 years to the "father" of the concept, Socrates, and it has grown to mean several types of thinking. Your understanding of this true definition will grow throughout this work, so let's start simply.

I believe critical thinking is stored in the brain in the same place as the will to live, the will to die and reasoning. All three require choice, by definition. To think is to compare A and B. To think critically, you must choose one or the other. Thinking is passive. Critical thinking is active. Advanced critical thinking involves thinking about an infinite number of options and choosing one. Thinking about writing a book is passive. Writing a book requires active advanced critical thinking. I think simple critical thinking is a reflex. Advanced critical thinking requires constant daily work and choices systematically cultivated.

Most of the discussion on critical thinking today is centered at American Universities and Colleges. Granted, many choose teaching over lucrative professions, for the passion of teaching more and more people, are realizing that well over 90% of teachers and administrators at these institutions are liberal and therefore biased in their thinking, writing and teaching. Critical thinking is also taught in college preparatory upper, middle and even lower levels. While the level of liberal thinking is nowhere near 90% at these institutions, it is certainly in the majority at upper levels though not as much in the lower school level. In the public school secondary level, the vast majority of teachers join the largest union in America, The National Education Association which overwhelmingly funds and endorses the liberal institutions and agenda at the national level.

What follows is my journey toward critical thinking, how it began, and grew exponentially over time. It is my hope that through this you will be led to understand critical thinking in your life and how you can best cultivate it.

At the outset, let me divulge that I have led a blessed life and have enjoyed unusually fertile ground in which to grow critical thinking thanks to my parents and relatively large family. I had two well educated, religious parents possessing ample wealth and resources to raise a family. I am keenly aware if you are missing any of these ingredients, the road to critical thinking can become immensely more difficult, but still not impossible. That being said, let's begin.

IN THE BEGINNING. . . .

I *was born William Colgan Tyler* (aka "Billy Boops"), at Norton's Infirmary, in Louisville, Kentucky, June 10, 1947. My father, Samuel Gwathmey Tyler, was born May 27, 1912, also in Louisville. His father died six months prior, and his mother, Edmonia Robinson, never remarried or bore any additional children. "B"(for baby) as my father was called, first attended all male, Male High School, and two years later attended all male, Culver Military Academy and graduated from Duke University in 1932. He married Claudia Tilford Colgan in 1936 after joining the Navy but prior to serving his WW II tour of duty in the Pacific, mostly on Guam. The couple lived in Palo Alto, California during the war returning to Louisville in 1942. It is interesting to note here that following the wedding ceremony, six years prior, there were two receptions—one at Edmonia's home and one at the Colgan home. Edmonia, not being overly social and believing that Claudia was not nearly good enough to marry her "B" (and no one was) refused to attend a reception.

Claudia T. Colgan, called "Coogie" by her friends, was born November 22, 1915 in Louisville, Kentucky to Claudia Tilford and William Colgan. She had one older brother, Robert T. Colgan, born four years prior. William Colgan, "Paw Paw," was born in 1870 and was previously married, but his wife and son both died in childbirth. He then married "Nanny" who was 15 years younger being born in 1885. They married in about 1909 when she was 24 and he was 39.

Coogie grew up on Crescent Avenue in Louisville, making many close friends with young debutantes her age. She was considered very attractive and quite humorous. She attended Atherton High School for Girls and later attended The University of Louisville briefly, but interrupted her studies to sail on a world cruise, chaperoned by her Uncle Henry C. Colgan and his wife in 1933 when she was 18.

But, I digress. When I was born, I was preceded by two older brothers, Gwathmey (aka "Squash") born five years earlier on July 2, 1942, and Robin (aka "Byrd") born two years prior on June 14, 1945. Younger brother Terry (aka "Terrible Terry") arrived three years later on May 5, 1950. Late September, early October was apparently prime breeding time in Louisville, especially for those seeking young males. We were all delivered at Norton's Infirmary in Louisville and lived in Anchorage, about 30 miles east toward Lexington. Brother Gwathmey was recently declared to be Anchorage's longest living resident at age 76.

ANCHORAGE

Anchorage was a bucolic burg of about 350 families when my parents moved there in 1942. Landmarks are Anchorage School, Kentucky Central Life Insurance Building—the town's only office building, across the L&N railroad tracks from the school, the Presbyterian Church to the west and the Presbyterian Orphanage further west. To the east of the Kentucky Central building are the U.S. Post Office, Anchorage Police Station and Fire Department. Back across the tracks is Saint Luke's Episcopal Church. Down the hill, to the north, are found the Anchorage Drug Store and Anchorage Grocery. About one mile north on Osage Road lies the Owl Creek Country Club, with a nine-hole golf course and swimming pool. Across Osage Road lies the 13-acre Tyler tract and stately two-story, Dutch Colonial house, sited approximately 150 yards from the road. Next door to the east is the home of Claudia's brother, Uncle Bob Colgan, his wife, Marie Castleman Colgan (Aunt Polly), and their three children; Robert T. Jr., born 1939; Polly C. Colgan, born 1941; and Marie (pronounced Mare-ree) S. Colgan, born 1946. Other residents at the Tyler home were three Irish Setters, Susie and daughters Sugar and Spice; Sheila, a black French poodle; a Welsh pony, Peewee; and a Tennessee Walking horse, Mal Arrive. Living at the Colgan home was Little Brother, a five-gaited saddle horse. Peewee formerly pulled a meat wagon around Louisville and the wagon was slowly decaying next to the two-stall barn, behind the house. Anchorage was noted for its large lots and homes and was originally settled as summer homes for Louisvillians, being at the end of the trolley car line. The town was named

Anchorage by its original settler, riverboat captain James W. Goslee in 1869, when he hung the anchor of his boat, the Matamora, inside of a locomotive wheel rim in the town square. Six years later, Aristides would win the first Kentucky Derby in 1875.

As stated at the outset, we all think. It is my belief that critical thinking is a part of human DNA, and it all depends on when and how you identify it, create the core and grow it. My core beliefs are rooted in a large immediate family and larger extended family wrapped by a small town. In that environment, everyone knows you, your brothers, parents etc. and you can never get away with anything. Anchorage, post WW II was leading the Baby Boomer growth with plenty of three-children families and a few four- and five-children families. There was only one family as I recall that had four boys and that was the Caldwells who lived about a third of a mile toward school. In age, they matched us year for year, except for the oldest who varied by one year. We were all good friends and our Dads both were elected to the Anchorage School Board, running together on the straight Sam ticket. Some of my first thoughts that I can remember before kindergarten are of close family and teachers that knew all my brothers.

Anchorage School Board, S. G. Tyler standing far right (no pun intended).

A particularly unique memory is of the Kindergarten Halloween costume competition when my mother, knowing this was her one and only shot, dressed me as the girl she always secretly wanted. Somehow, I escaped unbruised or traumatized. So much for the earliest memories. First grade at Anchorage School, remains a blur and a pain: Really tough, a lot to cover, and Mrs. Hall was not our favorite. The room was at the front of the school about as close as you could get to the railroad. About all I remember is Howard Oliver (I still don't know my name half the time) in his green jeans with suspenders (nobody wears suspenders). When a train came, maybe four times a day, he would jump to his feet and run to the window until it was gone, caboose included. Howard must have left town because I never saw him after first grade. I hope he is a train conductor!

MAINE

My next memory occurred the next summer before second grade in the summer of 1954. That was the summer of the first and maybe only family road trip to Maine of all places (three days). Picture four boys ages four, seven, nine and twelve in a four-door, unairconditioned station wagon with a luggage carrier on top. To avoid stopping every ten minutes, we instituted the T-T cup. The only way to hit the target without your brothers shoving and tickling you was for our parents to threaten the others with certain death. If you somehow completed the project, you handed the cup to Mom, where she, defying physics, would empty the cup while hurtling down the road at 60-70 mph. I do recall one, now famous stop when we pulled off the road after passing a mailbox labeled Agnes Ward, when all sons and Dad exited the car heading for the trees, and utilized what Mom begrudgingly dubbed the handiest tool at the picnic, while she squatted behind an open car door. Henceforth, in the future, when anyone needed to relieve themselves you went to see Agnes Ward. The first night we made it to Pittsburgh, Pennsylvania, where we stayed in our first ever overnight hotel. All I really remember was what Dad said was a steel mill, belching smoke and lighting the dark sky on the horizon. Up bright and early the next morning, we pointed the blue station wagon toward Upper Mont Claire, New Jersey. We were more experienced travelers now, trying not to be yelled at so much, but somehow the trip seemed longer and more boring. We made it to, and through, dinner and headed onto the final leg of Day 2. We were all dead asleep when the car finally came to a stop. We heard Dad rattling around the luggage and Mom began packing up the front seat. It was then she carefully pulled out a brown corrugated box from beneath her feet, which somehow had survived T-T cups and four small boys scrambling over seats to take turns sitting between Mom and Dad in the front. Mom, balancing the brown box, led the parade up the side walk and up three stairs to the front door lit by a porch light swarming with bugs. She rang the bell and we were greeted by loud shouts of welcome and two glasses of brown water and ice handed to Mom and Dad. The mysterious brown box was carefully opened to divulge a large yellow cake with caramel icing, none the worse for wear, prompting laughter, surprise and joy from all. We had arrived at the home of Barbara and Bill McCutcheon, long time WW II friends who had lived together in Palo Alto. We were quickly led through the potty and tooth brushing routine and whisked to cots and sleeping bags for the remainder of the short night. We learned the next morning that Mike, a year younger than Gwathmey, their oldest child, had already left for summer camp, and we were proudly introduced to daughter Linda, a year younger than Robin, and Billy, between my age and Terry's. After juice and a quick Danish, we said said Irish good-byes and backed slowly down the driveway. Dad, with his coffee tucked securely in his crotch, shifted through the three forward gears on the steering wheel column mounted stick shift and we were off to Day 3. Little did we know that we would see the McCutcheon's again in just four months when they qualified as valued first responders to our trauma coming up just around the corner. They would bring long cherished gifts from Cairn and Company, owned by Barbara's family and run now by Bill. Terry and I received official red metal fire helmets, just our size, emblazoned with our names and rank of chief. Gwathmey and Robin were given handsome leather belts and Mom and Dad received a large Leather Ice bucket with an American Eagle on the side, which donned their bar forever-after.

    The next morning, we watched as our station wagon was lashed to a very small ferry boat and we climbed aboard. For the next two hours Dad, the Navy veteran, watched anxiously as the boat pitched and rolled its way across the Sound with all his worldly possessions. We landed at North Haven, Maine, unlashed our car and headed to North Haven Lodge. Our accommodations were superb and included breakfast, lunch, and dinner. Staff and guests alike marveled at four boys, at our ages traveling that far or even at all for that matter. Dad would tell all that would listen that we had to leave four girls (dogs) at home with the neighbors. I also remember swimming in a large quarry where we caught an eel (yuck). The weather was cool, but the water was the coldest I had ever felt—including the ocean. The trip home was a repeat of the trip up, but even more boring.

BIRTHDAYS

Without *further ado let's* discuss the Tyler birthday tradition. Terry, May 5; Dad, May 27; Billy, June 10; Robin, June 14; Gwathmey, July 2; Mother, November, 22. With that number, with lavish celebrations, endless cards and voluminous gifts, no one would ever have been able to afford to go to college. Cake, ice cream, kiss, and unwrapped box of hand-me-downs was about all you could expect. No one was ever disappointed!

2ND GRADE BROUGHT POLIO

Back home after Labor Day, it was back to Anchorage School with Mrs. Haupt in the second grade. She lived in a house about a quarter of the way between our house and school, with her husband and older daughter, who was brother Gwathmey's age. Of course, she had taught both Gwathmey and Robin and told me, with the rest of the class listening, that I had some big shoes to fill. She was a kindly looking woman with a not so pretty mole on her chin.

On a day in about the middle of the month, I remember coming home from school being pretty tired. I actually fell asleep in my room and my mother had to waken me for dinner. After dinner, I was still tired and decided to go to bed early. When Mom tucked me in, she felt my forehead for a fever and commented I was a little warm, but we would see how I felt in the morning. When I awoke the next morning, I felt very tired and warm, and told Mom I didn't want to go to school. She felt my forehead again and told me to go back to sleep and she would check me again when she returned from taking my brothers to school. When she returned she was carrying a breakfast tray and thermometer. After taking my temperature, she frowned, told me eating something would make me feel better, and she was going to call Dr. Andrews. I dozed off after eating breakfast and she awakened me with a glass of water and a baby aspirin. The doctor said to call him in the morning with an update. By this time, I had to get up to go to the bathroom. I had difficulty straightening both legs and it was painful to walk. Somehow, I limped through the day, not feeling any better.

When I announced I didn't feel like coming down to the table for dinner, she said she would bring something after she fed the brothers. She came through as promised. After dinner, Gwathmey and Robin both came to my room and told me to quit faking and get back to school because Mom was acting concerned and was even getting irritable! I lied and promised to do what I could. When Mom came to give me more medicine and tuck me in, she presented my new summer friend—the T-T cup. She told me if I needed to poop, to call her and she would carry me to the john.

Next day, no better. After the update, the doctor said to bring me in, offering that it was probably the flu, but he wanted to run some tests. We were in his office after lunch. Two nurses wrestled me down screaming as they squeezed out a vile of blood. Upon personal observation and extending and contracting my legs painfully, the doctor said they should get the results in a few days and to continue the medication. He further advised that I be kept away from my brothers as much as possible. After we arrived home before dinner, four-year-old brother Terry moaned that he wasn't feeling so hot either. Again, Mom felt his forehead and promised he would get a formal temperature read after dinner, whereupon he was given a dose of aspirin and sent to bed early. Mom announced we likely would be switching up bedrooms tomorrow. Another doctor consult in the morning rendered an invitation for both me and Terry to go to the doctor the following day to review the results of my tests and to examine and test Terry. The next day I was feeling worse. It was too painful to extend my legs anywhere near a walking position and my shoulders and arms hurt as well. Terry complained of both leg and arm pain about equally.

Day 5. We arrived and Terry went through the same excruciating blood extraction process that I had except he had to donate two vials. After they returned Terry to Mom, they led me away to cough up another vial as well. When Dr. Harry Andrews entered the exam room he was greeted by two pale and pained little boys and their exhausted Mom. He pulled up a chair and began to extend and contract Terry's arms and legs inquiring with each movement the level of pain he felt. He then did the same with me. After writing notes on his notepad, he then turned to Mom. After praising our bravery and her patience and perseverance, he announced that the tests to date were inconclusive, but he was beginning to think what we were seeing was something called polio.

He added that he had seen a few cases and the hospitals were actually quite busy. The two extra blood vials were to be sent to a different lab that studied mostly polio. Mom admitted to having heard of polio, but would like more information. She declared that she had not heard of any cases with our friends or from any of her friends. He said he wanted to discuss the findings with some of his colleagues and other specialists. He instructed her on the way out to check with his nurse and she would give her prescriptions for each of us and a few sheets of information on polio. The next steps would include visits to an orthopedic surgeon and physical therapists which he would facilitate. At this time, it was too early estimate the depth or duration of this disease for either of us. We could be put in the same bedroom for now and should have only minimal contact with the rest of the family and visitors. We headed home tired, bewildered and confused. I would not see the inside of the second-grade classroom at Anchorage School again.

WHAT IS IT?

A *brief primer on polio may* be helpful here. There are three basic types—non-paralytic, paralytic, and bronchial. Non-paralytic usually causes fever, some nausea, limb muscle pain, and is gone in about a week with no residual effects. Paralytic, our type, starts with fever, limb muscle pain, overall weakness and malaise. Duration and residual effects vary. Bronchial is likely the worst because it affects the lungs, and is treated by putting the patient in an iron lung machine to assist breathing. Bronchial likely causes the most deaths. Records indicate there were approximately 35,000 registered polio cases in the U.S. in 1954, down from 54,000 in 1953. The vaccine was relatively widely distributed in 1955 and by 1959, newly reported cases fell to 500. In Louisville, 198 cases were reported in 1954. We knew one person and friend who had bronchial polio and after exiting the iron lung, was paralyzed from the neck down and restricted to a wheelchair the rest of his life. There was some talk that he was predicted not to live past his early twenties. He is still alive today with a wife and three children. More about Chase Forrester later. Perhaps the most famous polio victim was FDR. He contracted the disease at about age 30, became severely depressed and an alcoholic. It was not until he went for treatment to Warm Springs, Georgia, and saw the remarkable dedication and progress of the young patients there that he shed his self-pity and made real improvement.

It turns out that polio is a very contagious virus but no one to my knowledge ever figured out how it was transmitted. Many assumed it was through swimming pools, but that was never proven. I knew of only one other case in Anchorage. A young girl about Terry's age who lived nearby was stricken in both legs. Dr. Jonas Salk isolated the virus and Dr. Sabin figured out how to administer it via a sugar cube. Since there were three types of polio, even if you contracted one type you needed to be protected from the other two. In the U.S. polio seemed to be more prevalent during the flu season, the reason being it was easier to contract when the immune system was already compromised. The reason Polio has not been fully eradicated is that in primitive societies you build up natural immunities when the community bathes, urinates and defecates in the community water supply. When modern purification and plumbing arrives, the immunity protection is removed and humans become susceptible to the virus.

Back at the home front Terry and I settled into the two single beds in the largest bedroom, adjacent to our parents. Robin and Gwathmey settled into the two single beds in the bedroom next to our adjoining bath. That left the guestroom available for Nanny who became a more frequent guest and caregiver. That pretty well filled our four-bedroom, two-bath upstairs. Dad, who had likely been away on a business trip, returned to the sickroom to pass some love around, give us a pep talk and instructions to be a thoughtful of Mom as possible. He gave a similar talk in the next bedroom. Dad was employed as an industrial finishes salesman in the Robertson Paint Company in downtown Louisville, about 30 miles away. His clients were heater, air conditioner, stove, refrigerator, washer and dryer manufacturers. Since all of his clients were not in Louisville, it required him to take week-long road trips about once a month, plus the annual furniture mart every February in Hickory, North Carolina. Eventually he drove over a million miles, was a very skilled driver, and loved cars.

The next couple of weeks were pretty well consumed by doctor visits. Dr. Armond Fischer, orthopedic surgeon, was the next stop. He stretched our arms and legs, tested our strength in each in all directions, measured length of each and circumference of each. He took extensive notes. He wrote a prescription for orthotics for each, for medication and treatments. The orthotic prescription was sent to the brace company and we were to receive those in a couple of weeks. Next stop was the physical therapist, Dr. Carson. He did his own exam and then introduced us both to our own whirlpool bath. Finally, a little fun and relief. Lastly, we returned to Dr. Andrews, pediatrician, for a summary, final instructions and to answer any remaining questions. The decision, due in part to crowded conditions at the hospital and ample coverage at home was primarily home therapy and treatment.

TREATMENT BEGINS

Back home we awaited results. In a few days, a large, stainless steel kettle with a top and wheels was wheeled in, placed at the foot of my bed, and a separate plug was secured. The next morning the nurses arrived and the Taco-Torture was about to begin. First, they loaded two blue wool blankets into the kettle, now filled with water and commenced to bring them nearly to a boil. Then, they spread a rubber mat onto each bed. When the blankets reached the proper temperature, they wrapped Terry and me into rubber mats. Next, they wrapped each of us in the wet blankets that had first been sent thru a wringer, and finally wrapped each of us in another rubber mat. "Whoo-wee" that was hot and that wet wool itched something terrible with no way to scratch it. After about 30-45 minutes of cooking, everything was removed, we toweled down and put our pajamas back on. Following that, our arms and legs were raised, lowered and stretched. The stretching, despite the heating was very painful. Each day we measured how much we further we had stretched the limb with the maximum allowable pain. Each day they would hold it longer in the most painful position and time it. I am not exactly sure all what the neighbors heard. After both nurses and Mom were trained, one would come in the morning and one in the afternoon with Mom assisting. This went on for six days a week. Eventually the braces arrived and were fitted. Terry received a right leg brace up to his knee and a corset-based device holding supports for both arms. Rubber balls were installed at the end of each arm extension so he would not inadvertently poke out a friend's eye. I received a left leg brace all the way up my thigh and a right leg brace up to my knee. My right arm was slightly affected but did not require a brace since I did not walk on my arms. Actually, however, part of our later therapy involved someone picking up of our feet and walking on our hands for longer and longer periods. Difficult for me, but very tough for Terry. For some unknown reason polio always strikes transversely or entirely, but with varying effects. Attempting longer and longer walks were added to our daily regimen. Depending on our progress and growth rate, the braces would need to be adjusted. Eventually the blankets were discarded and replaced by what was called chemically enhanced heat packs, much like what is still used by therapists today, still initially heated in warm water. As we improved, one of the twice daily taco wraps was replaced by a 30-minute soak in a hot tub. Such became the daily routine that would continue throughout the end of the year and into the first quarter of 1955.

Once we got settled in, the visits from my parents' friends and the neighbors began—nearly all bearing gifts, some even for my brothers. The early stream was several a week, but it trailed off after a month or so, but picked up over the holidays. We were restricted to our beds, assisted only by a bed pan and T-T cup. The older brothers were generally sympathetic, but Robin got pretty jealous of all the attention. Sometimes our presents got diverted to or stolen by him. We had a black and white TV downstairs in the den that got two channels. Terry and I became a rare, juvenile breed of radio fan. The Breakfast Club with Don McNeal from a hotel in Chicago, Our Gal Sunday, the Arthur Godfrey Show, the Lone Ranger, Amos and Andy, Cisco Kid, Grand ole Opry, Lux Radio Theater, Ma Perkins, One Man's Family, Our Miss Brooks, Perry Mason, The Roy Rogers Show, Young Doctor Malone. This allowed me a one-time opportunity to develop an imagination with horses clomping on a road, door squeaking open, closing etc.

NANNY

And then there is our incredible Nanny, Mother's mother. At some stage, she started making regular visits from in town, spending the night in the guest bedroom to let Mom and Dad take a well needed break and get out of the house. She would say our prayers with us every night, sometimes read, and nearly always recount a tale that Brer Rabbit had shared with her when she rounded the last curve by Owl Creek Country Club on the way to our house. They were endless—many, I am sure from the book, but even more from her incredible imagination. She sat in a large rocker, her silhouette outlined by the light beaming in from the bathroom. The rocker had a slight squeak which sang us to sleep. What is a young critical mind thinking right about now? First, pain, shock and awe. Then an orderly process began to take hold. It is rare that anyone so young, can step off the merry-go-round of life and begin to watch it go by. It suddenly all begins to rotate around you. Soo...this is what friends and neighbors do. This is who doctors are and what hospitals are for. But at the same time, I felt a sense of loss that I could not walk! I was now different from everyone else. How long would this last? I had my first inkling that in just an instant, something very important—something that everyone has—can be taken away from you, out of the blue and through no fault of your own. You start looking at all the gifts people have that everyone takes for granted. At times, it will make me angry, how many people have no concept of this. So, you begin to live each day, thankful to be alive and for all that you DO have. Two loving parents that have the ability, patience and resources to care for you. A younger brother in the next bed to go through this together with and two older brothers to beat sense and reality into your head. It struck me later in life, that polio was a unique disease in that it usually strikes the young and takes them off the merry-go-round to begin to reflect and appreciate life for what it is. The life success rate of polio "victims" is consistently high and in many instances extraordinary (through no fault of their own). Not to mention polio will definitely keep you off the battlefield!

So, what do you do about continuing an education? Terry was just beginning to learn how to read so Mom and Nanny would conduct classes daily and help him work through workbook assignments. For me, Mom got second grade textbooks and workbooks from Mrs. Haupt, the second grade teacher, and made sure I did daily assignments that she would grade and correct. Eventually Mrs. Haupt came over for some private tutoring sessions.

EASTER DEBUT

B*y now, spring was springing,* and we were evidencing increasing progress with walking and stamina. It was Sunday, April 10, 1955 and it was decided everyone would attend Easter Sunday services at St. Luke's Episcopal Church in Anchorage (our first church service since September). Here is the scene: walking down the aisle, Gwathmey first, Robin second, me third—with my long brace up to my thigh on my left leg and short brace on my right leg. Then came Terry, sporting a short brace on his right leg and wearing a corset contraption with steel bars extending strait out from his shoulders with rubber balls at the ends and slings, attached by springs holding his outstretched arms, not unlike a scarecrow. Mom and Dad brought up the rear. We clambered into our pew, with Terry shuffling sideways and given ample arm room. When the processional hymnal was sung, there was hardly a dry eye in the place, but accompanied by a few wry smiles. To this day, I cannot get through an Easter Service with a dry eye.

Later that month we experienced a very special treat. Mary Martin was debuting in Peter Pan on color TV and our neighbors, the Bromleys, invited the whole family over to watch it on their new color set. They provided drinks, which we spilled, and snacks, and we got to stay up late. Truly memorable in a repetitively dull existence.

The study, exercise and walk routine continued throughout the spring and early summer. At some point foot boards were installed in our beds. Our task was to push the heel down to the board and hold it as long as bearable. It was very painful, but we eventually made acceptable progress which was gratifying. At another point balloons were strung over our beds where we had to do high, straight leg kicks to hit the balloons. Again, difficult and painful but we got through it.

The summer break allowed Mrs. Haupt to increase her tutoring schedule with me to three days a week at the beginning of June. After a rigorous month for both of us, Mrs. Haupt was prepared to recommend me for entry into the third grade, subject to my completion of the summer reading list over the rest of the summer.

CAPE MAY, NEW JERSEY AND THE CHALFONTE HOTEL

What came next was probably the best prescription any doctor has ever written for any patient. In the late spring, Dr. Fischer announced after our visit that the best therapy for us at this point would be walking in the sand on a beach for as long as my parents could afford it. Louisville and even "summer cottage" Anchorage, had oppressive, Ohio River valley heat in the summer. The question for my parents was where? Most of Louisville spent summer vacation in northern Michigan, not on the Atlantic shore. We all knew Maine was too far. After consulting a map, it was decided the closest beach location would be a two day car trip to southern New Jersey. After a number of inquiries, it was decided to stay at an old boarding house called the Chalfonte Hotel in Cape May. All four boys would go and spend all of July and August with Mom. Dad would drive us all up in the "family-truckster" with the luggage rack on top, settle us in for a few days, return at the end of August for a week and bring us home.

Off we went. After Maine, we were veterans, all eager to see Agnes Ward again along the way. After two long days, we arrived in the dark of night. Terry and I were carried to our beds and Robin and Gwathmey followed. Mom tucked us in bed while Dad unloaded the car and checked in. We were awakened in the morning and gathered to go down to the dining room. We were greeted in the lobby by Mrs. Satterfield, the owner, who escorted us toward our table. After entering the large dining hall and arriving at our table, we were greeted by another woman who escorted the children to the "children's dining room" just past the other end of the main hall. Mom said she would check on us shortly. We had a great breakfast and were assisted by the mostly black kitchen staff. After breakfast, back to our room, changed into our swim suits, donned sun screen and went searching for the beach.

The Chalfonte built in 1870, reached its peak in the 1920's and as we learned on the guided horse drawn carriage tour years later, it is where all the southern drunks stayed. It is 100 rooms plus a couple of out cottages. Three stories, unairconditioned, non-elevatored, all wood Victorian fire trap, three blocks from the Atlantic Ocean and wrapped on two levels with rocker lined porches on both the Howard and Franklin Street sides. One out cottage is on Franklin Street along with the Tin House, men's and women's beach showers with the requisite peep hole for the not yet educated. It was currently owned by the Satterfield family from Richmond, Virginia, who had bought it from the builder/owner Captain Sawyer. Grandmother Satterfield or Mini, as her age-group called her, managed the place with the help of her old crony, Mrs. Nash, who when asked how she was feeling each morning would wryly smile and moan, "No better, no better." The assistant manager was Anne LeDuc, a woman who in the winter coached girls' field hockey at The George School in Pennsylvania, was my mother's age, and soon became Mom's and our best friend. Mini Satterfield's children and grandchildren would arrive at the same time each year, which was shortly, and stay for a month. The remainder of the desk staff and night watchmen were young college guys. The wait staff in the dining room was mostly college girls with the exception of two young black men who were from Richmond and worked for the Satterfields. The head cook in the kitchen was Helen assisted by her daughter Dorothy, who wintered in Richmond. The head handyman was a black man named Theodore who was either from Richmond or Cape May. He lived in a small locked room and could be found most nights in a chair behind the kitchen puffing on his pipe, which I learned years later when I worked at the hotel was filled with marijuana. He was in charge of the Sunday night clam bakes and beach parties. The head bellman was a stately, elderly black man also from Richmond, who, when asked if the hotel had a set of encyclopedias in the library, would reliably respond, "No, but what is it you would like to know?"

The majority of the guests were annuals who appeared every year at the same time and always stayed the same amount of time, in the same room each year. Most came from Richmond, the Philadelphia, environs, or the New York City area. Most were adults who sometimes brought children and or grandchildren. We had a suite of three rooms on the second floor that shared a common bath. Most of the rooms were without baths but maybe had a sink. Bathrooms and showers were on the hallways. Our suite was just down the hall from the owner's suite. She didn't care much for crying children and we did our best to stay out of the way. Our suite opened onto a second-floor porch with rockers. Each room was entered through a louvered door, like a western bar door, that locked on the inside with a metal hook. These doors were designed to facilitate air flow and there were no keys. You could store any valuables in the safe in the lobby.

The daily routine which we quickly fell into was breakfast in the morning, then off to the beach, returning for lunch at 1:00 followed by a nap. Then back to the beach at 3:00 or 4:00 returning for a bath or shower at 5:30, and 6:30 dinner. Adults would often assemble for cocktails at 6:00 to 6:30 on the porch, outside of our room, and sometimes continue at the "tin house" behind the hotel, postponing dinner to last call at 7:30. Adults wore coats and ties to dinner; children, not so fancy. There was usually a sitter for us after dinner in the children's dining room until the adults finished dinner. An iron clad rule that we often forgot was NO running in the dining room, not a particular problem in the early years for me and Terry, but a common violation for Gwathmey and Robin. As stated earlier, the beach was three blocks from the hotel. The first year, due to Terry's and my condition, we either drove or were driven to the beach. The first year was the first time any of us had been to an ocean beach. The beach was lined with tents for shade and beach chair storage. They were mostly unused during the week, but filled up with rent payers on the weekend with the workers from Philly and NYC. Cape May surf was very robust as was the undertow. Every 200 to 300 yards was a two-man life guard station, with life boats nearby. Every few hours, if it hadn't occurred naturally, there was a life guard drill when after a number of whistle tweets, they would go running down the beach, launch a boat and head out in the ocean where thy would remain for about an hour, just beyond the swimmers, and then return. Very well trained and disciplined team. You really felt very safe. These were well paid college guys who attracted a bevy of bikinied, bronze beach babes around each chair. Gwathmey and Robin were good swimmers and took immediately to body surfing. Terry and I not so fast. We played and waded along the edge and became experts in early castle design and construction. We dug through sand to water and much later learned that the dark layer was oil deposits caused by northeastern industrial shipping lanes. We buried each other up to our heads in sand and threatened abandonment. Later in the summer, we both became strong and more venturesome, getting a good work out every day.

On the 4th of July, we were invited to go on a small ferry boat from the nearby harbor to watch the fireworks. As it got dark and the fire-works commenced, Terry began to cry almost hysterically, and my mother slapped him across the face which shocked him into silence. A woman sitting next to Mom, leaned over and said, "thanks, I was about to do that for you!" Needless to say, the summer passed quickly and before we knew it, Dad arrived and we were headed back home.

LOUISVILLE HISTORY

This may be a good spot to give a quick history of Louisville. Louisville came into existence primarily because of the falls in the Ohio River and the need to portage around them. The next city up stream was Cincinnati, Ohio. Rivers were the early interstates and they attracted all sorts of businesses and events. When the Civil War came in 1860, Louisvillians fought on both sides, brother against brother. My great, great grandfather, John Colgan, started a drug store with 100% borrowed money at 18, just as the war broke out, and somehow managed to repay it all in two years. He eventually started a chain of four stores despite spending two years in prison in Memphis for being a Southern sympathizer. A chemist, John was the first to put sugar in cough syrup, and later is credited with inventing chewing gum by adding sugar to chicle that was imported from South America as a cheap substitute for rubber for automobile tires. This was about the same time as another drug store chemist was inventing Coca-Cola just south in Atlanta. The chewing gum was labeled Colgan's Taffy Tu-Lu and packaged as chips in small tins like snuff. The product sold throughout the U.S., Canada and Australia. It was the first product packaged with baseball cards primarily because Louisville was granted the first National League baseball franchise with the Louisville Sluggers. Following quickly came the formation of Hillerich and Bradsby, the manufacturer of Louisville Slugger Baseball bats. Not to miss out on all the excitement, the first Kentucky Derby was run in 1875, won by Aristides. Just when John was preparing to mechanize his manufacturing process, the city fathers came begging him not to, as it was not a good time to lay off workers. The company was soon sold in the early 1900's to a company that eventually became the American Chicle Company, the first user of billboards which appeared on the railroad from Washington to New York. As usual, the winner is the best marketer, not the inventor. The John Colgan gum fortune never made it to the second generation.

The main products that Louisville eventually became most noted for were tobacco (Reynolds Tobacco), Bourbon Whiskey (Brown-Forman, Pappy Van Winkle), The Kentucky Derby, fast horses and beautiful women (or vice-versa). Just like the good Southern river towns of New Orleans, Birmingham and Memphis, Louisville took to introducing its beautiful women at about age 18 to the broader population through gala debutante parties. The tradition continues to this day (albeit diminished). In the early 1950s, all these cities had to make some hard decisions about growth. The Louisville City fathers (perhaps selfishly) decided that they didn't need all the troubles that they felt rapid growth might bring. Of course, the City Fathers already owned all the major companies, including the city newspapers, the morning "Courier Journal" and evening "Louisville Times," owned by the liberal Bingham family. As we all know, Atlanta won the growth prize with the Atlanta airport, and the final quality of life jury is still out.

THE TYLER ESTATE

While *we are still* in the descriptive mode let's take a quick tour of the Tyler house, grounds and outbuildings in Anchorage. As you stand on the front porch you gaze over 200 yards of green grass front yard ending on Osage Road and Owl Creek Country Club clubhouse. The Osage Road frontage is bordered by a white-washed wooden fence about five feet tall. The paved driveway ascends a slight hill, turning left in front of the house making a circle on itself and back out. A connected paved parking space lies at the base of five wide concrete stairs leading to an open concrete porch along the entire front of the house with the front door in the middle. Entering the front hall with a ten-foot ceiling, you are greeted by a large living room on the right and dining room on the left. Going straight down the hall past these entry ways you meet three stairs leading to a large landing (large enough to fit two large sleeping dogs) with steps leading upstairs to the left. Continuing with the landing on the left, a small den is to your right, coat closet and bathroom straight ahead and the kitchen to the left. Both the living room and den have wood-burning fireplaces. Through the den is a small concrete side porch, seldom used. Entering the kitchen from the hall, take a right to exit to the wooden back utility porch, with a maid's room (with bed, metal shower, sink and commode). The back covered porch serves as a shelter for firewood and is used for children's dining in the summer. Re-entering the relatively small kitchen, turn right to the sink. Left from the sink the swinging door leads back into the dining room and to the right of the swinging door is the small breakfast room and washer/dryer. Exit the breakfast room on the left and enter a covered porch also accessed from the dining room and exit back onto the front porch. Across from the breakfast room to the left of the swinging door is a door leading down a flight of wooden stairs with a handrail on the left open side. At the bottom is the furnace. Circling left under the stair we see water heaters, a sump pump, utility sink and a metal table facilitating the nightly feeding of the dogs rotating weekly among the four brothers, depending on health and attendance. Turning right at the furnace, ducking your head slightly to avoid bumping into a large duct, you enter a large rectangular room, longer at the right. On your right is a 4x8 green plywood table, followed by another 4x8 green plywood table, attached to another plywood table forming an L breaking to the left.

THE TRAIN

Dad, Gwathmey, and to a lesser extent Robin had been busy on their own little project over the last nine months as Terry and I sucked up almost all the parental love battling the ravages of polio.

Dad attempted to balance the scale, and save his own sanity by building not one, but two train sets. The primary set was a full scale Lionel special. It featured two meandering tracks, one inside the other, connected by two switches, powered by a two-handled transformer, each controlling energy to its own track and located at the apex of the L. The engineer, standing at the transformer, handle in each hand, commandeered two trains, either on one or two tracks at the same time turning his head left and right constantly to catch all the action. It was like standing on one leg, chewing gum, rubbing your belly with one hand and patting your head with the other. A definite challenge for a growing boy recovering from polio! We had two very heavy, black locomotives, one larger than the other and each a coal car and caboose. In between were a large number of interchangeable utility cars, enclosed box cars including milk car with automatic unloader and platform, flat bed timber car with its separate loader and unloader, search light car, and maintenance cars. In addition, we had a bright red, Santa Fe, forward and rear-facing diesel passenger engine with its own lighted passenger cars and caboose. And finally, we had a separate trolley car that changed direction when it struck a bumper with its front or rear. Over the years we added grass, trees and village buildings. Partially to keep Robin distracted and give him needed experience, a second table was added when he got bored with some of the tedious tasks required to make the main set operational. This second set was the same gauge as the first, and laid out in a simple figure eight. The engine was light weight metal and there were several light weight cars. It was very durable and had its own small transformer. It was truly a starter set that we enjoyed wrecking time and again. When Terry and I became more mobile we eagerly awaited our turn at each transformer. Both provided endless hours of entertainment.

What a tribute to critical thinking! Dad spent valuable time and money with two sons to build a train set enjoyed by four for over 20 years cumulative. All from a man who had no father, no brothers and no sisters. The trains are still set up and running and fought over by both brothers and cousins.

Leaving the room, we see the fourth green 4x8 table located in front of a curved-glass china cabinet filled with antique family stemware and china. This table is to become covered in blood and sweat from the ping-pong wars to be fought among the brothers, parents, neighbors, friends and relatives. The china cabinet came within inches of the backswing of a smashing forehand and was practically in the broader field of play during doubles matches. The fact that this edifice remained undamaged is one of many Tyler boy miracles!

Climbing back upstairs we exit the back porch descending three concrete stairs onto a smooth loose river gravel descending patio. Up by the door stands a white wooden post on which is mounted a large iron dinner bell rung to announce dinner and other important assemblages across the seemingly vast back and side yards. Off to the left lies a wire mesh fence dividing our lot from the neighboring Eggers' farm. George Egger owned several businesses in Louisville and was married to crazy Helen. The Eggers raised cattle, a few horses and loud guinea hens. It presented a pleasant pastoral setting. Unfortunately, one afternoon, a couple of our dogs dug under the fence and got into the hen house causing quite a ruckus ending in two loud gunshots. Dad walked to the fence and summoned Helen who ambled up to the fence carrying a double-barrel shotgun. He leaned across the fence grabbing the gun from Helen, whereupon she slapped him across the face. He then summoned the dogs who crawled back under the fence with tails between their legs, and returned to the house, gun in hand, dogs in tow. We never, ever stepped foot on the Egger property.

To the right of the patio lies a white lattice work structure housing a pump house surrounded by a wooden bin housing metal trash cans. Continuing on to the right, a short sidewalk extends to meet a section of paved driveway attached to the entry circle. This is the spot reserved for the garbage man, J.B. Smith; the dry-cleaning man, Al Buman; the milk man, Luther Hinkle; the builder/handy man; and other service providers to access the rear of the house. The driveway extends, unpaved, down a slight hill, past a small cottage to the barn-stable-garage, large enough to provide for a horse, large pony, three cars and a decaying wooden wagon previously pulled by the pony delivering meat around Louisville. Now the cottage served as a home to a considerable number of guests over time. The first were Fritz and Ajayneya who, we think were indentured servants Dad won in card game at Owl Creek. He drove a vintage, needle nose Studebaker car and did odd jobs around our house. She did laundry and some babysitting. They spoke very little English and lasted about two years. Next came Winston Blackley, Dad's first cousin from Memphis, who stayed about a year. Last came the reptile house, initiated and maintained by Terry and Harry Macy. More about Winston and Harry Macy later. The only other structure is a small wooden playhouse slightly left of the back door, filled with all sorts of tricycles, bicycles, yard tools and small mowers. White slat fencing, matching that in the front, extends from the Egger farm, behind the playhouse, down to the cottage, past the barn-stable-garage, turning left a short way, and then left again to reconnect with the Egger property. This, plus three service gates, create ample, pleasant, serviceable pastureland for the livestock. All of the land extending to the right and rear of the house all the way to the Colgan's house comprises about 12 acres. Hence the most oft repeated phrase of both parents: "There are 13 acres out there, now get off your lazy butts and go out there and enjoy them."

FIRST RESPONDERS

B*efore returning to the* fairly routine daily schedule, my parents' good friends and first responders to this family-wide wreck require a brief introduction. Mostly my mother's best friends and families were Aunt Kitty and Uncle Bill Harrison, Aunt Katie and Uncle Van Van Winkle, Aunt Nancy and Uncle Jeff Stewart, and Aunt Ella and Uncle Donald Dinning. Aunt Kitty, Aunt Katie, Aunt Nancy and sometime substitute Aunt Ella and Mother comprised the core of the soon to be dreaded bridge group. They lunched and played bridge all Tuesday afternoon and it sometimes grew into two tablesful. They rotated weekly among each other's houses. When we arrived home when it was Mother's week, we often saw her sitting with a white lace handkerchief on her head, signaling luck had not been coming her way. We used to snicker when Mother would tell us to scram because they had several more rubbers to play. Mother, Aunt Kitty and Aunt Katie had all made their debut together. The Harrisons lived in town, had a couple of boys that went away to school, but we shot dove occasionally and their father died of a heart attack after shooting a double—the very finest way to die. Aunt Katie and Uncle Van lived in town, had three children,—Sally, Gwathmey's age; Kitty, Robin's age; and Julian, Terry's age. The girls were beautiful. Gwathmey dated Sally a little and Robin dated Kitty some (I said in my toast at Robin's wedding rehearsal dinner which almost got me thrown out of the family –"he wined and dined, cooed and wooed her, but I don't think he ever sc.......d her... Don't you think it would be clever, if I switched from this endeavor?......" Aunt Nancy and Uncle Jeff lived in

Anchorage and we always spent New Year's Day watching football games at their house. They had two children, Nancy, older than Gwathmey, and Jeff, who was Robin's age. He went away to boarding school and to college at Harvard. Aunt Ella and Uncle Donald had two older nephews, lived in Anchorage, and Donald was a judge and legal counsel to Anchorage School. I don't think there were three prettier ladies in Louisville than Mom, Aunt Katie and Aunt Nancy.

3ᴿᴰ GRADE BEGINS

Tanned, rested and ready, the first day back at Anchorage School in Mrs. Mitchell's third grade was a little scary, stressful and tiring. Everybody was very welcoming but I had a lot of "'splainin'" to do to fill everybody in. Lots of questions, not all with answers, plus a lot of academic catching up to do. Take it a day at a time. I was beginning to learn my limitations in comparison to my classmates. I was not anyone's first pick as a team mate, was spastic, and had not played most sports at all. Frankly, I was getting depressed, and for the first time feeling sorry for myself. Mom saw it right away and started the pep talks, and Dad started getting home earlier after work in time for some pitch and catch and batting practice before dinner and dark. But slowly, I got on top of the wave academically, and could see some progress physically. The teachers and coaches were patient. Choir practice started and I actually had a somewhat decent voice.

THANKSGIVING

B*efore I knew it,* it was Thanksgiving. Thanksgiving dinner was always at our house with all the Colgans plus Nanny in attendance. The children's table overflowed from the dining room into the entry hall. Dad in sport coat and tie always carved the turkey on the dining room sideboard patiently giving lessons to all the brothers when they achieved the appropriate age, about 12, and Gwathmey, passing his test last year, was assistant this year. Paw-Paw, Mom's father, had died the previous October at age 85 having spent two plus years in the Pee Wee Valley Old Age Sanitarium about ten miles west of Anchorage. We had visited him several times there even with our busy polio schedule.

CAVE HILL CEMETERY

The weekend after Thanksgiving Day we always made time to visit Cave Hill Cemetery in Louisville where all the known relatives were buried. Everyone attended this year, even Mom who attended infrequently. She came this year because we were laying a wreath on Paw Paw's new grave for the first time.

Dad had attended Male High School for boys which played their archrival Manual High School the Friday after Thanksgiving every year. They gave their girlfriend a white mum emblazoned with a purple M and wrapped in a purple ribbon. At Cave Hill Dad lovingly placed a fresh mum, just like that on Edmonia's headstone. The mum and evergreen wreaths for many of the other markers were picked up at Nanz and Kraft Florists just outside the gates of Cave Hill. The Tyler Plot was started when my great, great, great grandfather Levi Tyler died in 1861 at 76 having been born in 1789. His passing is noted on a large four-sided obelisk near the center of the plot. Two as yet unborn second cousins would bear his name. Levi was preceded by Edward born 1767 and Edward begat Henry Samuel Tyler in 1815 (Mayor of Louisville at the time of his death) who begat Isaac in 1838 and Isaac begat Samuel Gwathmey, who died and begat Samuel Gwathmey Tyler, Jr. in 1912.

After wandering the plot, marveling at all the names and dates, Dad began telling short stories about his recollections of nearly a dozen notables. At some juncture I wandered onto a nearby plot, looked down and read the name William Colgan and ran back to Dad inquiring why MY name was on the nearby stone.

He told the story of Paw Paw's first wife who died in childbirth and that son was named William Colgan. We then got back in the car drove by several plots of other close relatives eventually arriving at the newer section of the cemetery and Mother placed a wreath on her father's new headstone. Finally, we returned to the center of the old section back near the Tyler plot to the large lake where we fed bread crumbs to the ducks, swans and geese. We left with my head spinning in amazement with all the relatives and how many years we had lived in Louisville.

CHRISTMAS 1955

Back to school, a little studying, Christmas plays and concerts, and it was time for Christmas again. Like most other things, the Tylers do things differently. We get our Christmas tree in the late afternoon on Christmas Eve. Down to the grocery store tree lot, across the street from the drug store. There are about three trees left. It was only later that we learned they leave the scrawniest till last....and they are also the cheapest. The fab four boys tie the tree to the top of the station wagon while Dad negotiates for the last penny. Proudly we make the short trip home to show Mom. Upon arrival, we pull the tree up the front porch stairs, into the far end of the living room in front of the window, hoist it into its stand, straighten it, and call Mom. She enters the room with the first of the ornament boxes and proclaims it is the prettiest tree we have ever had. The first task is to test the lights and replace the damaged ones. We were a colored light tree family and Dad made certain they were strung to high standards. Many little hands assisted and only after a unanimous light approval, ornament hanging began, with each son in charge of hanging his favorites on the side of the tree where Santa would place their presents later that night, while the parents continued to make numerous trips to the attic to retrieve more ornaments. Shortly, Mom calls us to dinner in the dining room across the hall. After dinner, a little more ornament hanging, then off to an early bed time reading of "The Night before Christmas" and we all fight sugar plumbs in our head struggling to drop off to sleep.

As you might expect, we awoke very early. I open one eye to see if Terry is awake yet. Not yet. I spot a Christmas Stocking tied to the end of my bed that Santa must have brought. I opened several small presents inside and emptied out all the candy. I sneak up to Terry's ear whispering "Terry" until he wakes up. Then I go in the next bedroom and awaken Robin and Gwathmey. They roll over and grumble. I then go back to my room. After waiting a few minutes, I return and announce to Robin and Gwathmey that Terry and I are going in to awaken Mom and Dad. Terry and I go into our snoring parents' room, me standing on the bed side with my father and Terry with my Mother. We then shake them saying it is time to see Santa! Not much reaction. Mother then asks if Robin and Gwathmey are up yet, to which I answer in the affirmative. She tells us to go to our room, put on our robe and slippers and she and Dad will be in a minute. We return to our rooms, I pass the instructions on to my older brothers and return to my room to don robe and slippers. Mom appears shortly, still tying her robe and tells us to line up in the hallway, don't dare start downstairs, and she will be right back with Dad. We do as told, and soon hear water running and toilet flushing in the parents' bathroom. Mom then reappears going to the head of the line and announces she will lead us downstairs to start breakfast and Dad will be down shortly. We moan in unison "breakfast?" following her downstairs, she announcing on the way, "no looking in the living room!" Once assembled in the breakfast room, the milk, juice, and cold cereal added, the coffee perked and finally Dad appears. Acquiescing to unanimous appeals, he relents, and we line up, youngest first, to march into the living room, singing Happy Birthday to Jesus, the final refrain replaced "ooohs, aahhs," and acclamations of joy as we spotted our most coveted requests. Plus, the tree looked totally different because it was now covered in tinsel. What an amazing Santa Claus!

    To be regretfully honest, this year's presents completely faded with the largess of the first responders' gifts that recently preceded them. As best I can recall some of the biggest hits were a tricycle for Terry, bicycle for me, and train set additions for Gwathmey and Robin. Mom then dutifully chronicled on a yellow legal pad the list of gifts from friends and relatives as we shouted them out and she reminded us to make sure we kept each card with the gift. Garbage bags filled and required removal. All the while, Dad dutifully tended blazing fires in both the den and living room and Bing Crosby and Perry Como softly sang Christmas Carols in the background.

The yellow pad quickly began to fill with the list of regulars. Each son had two godfathers and one godmother. My godmother was Jane Bailey, a cousin and friend of Mom's living in Zanesville, Ohio, with husband Buck (who spoke with a slight speech impediment mocked perfectly by Robin) and their two daughters, Claudia and Elenore, names which were unfortunate because in Buck (and Robin's) lingo, "L" became "R". (Try saying those names aloud quickly without laughing!) My godfathers were Uncle Jeff Stewart and Dick Smith, a neighboring Anchorageite and golfing buddy of Dad's. He was married to Sue Todd, Louisville grown girl and sometimes Tuesday bridge sub, and they had two sons Ricky (a little younger than Gwathmey) and Billy (my age) and daughter Linda (Robin's age). The Cheek family (Louisvillians with older girls) would send us each socks, annually, moanfully announced by one and dittoed simultaneously by all. Dad's Aunt Marguerite Blackley, Edmonia's sister, lived in Memphis, Tennessee, with her two sons Norman and Winston. Norman, lifelong bachelor, car collector and boat builder, would sometimes send one practical gift to be used by all, WD-40, Windshield antifreeze and jumper cables come to mind. I am sure there is another whole list of friends and relatives with older children that have binding reciprocal no gift contracts with my parents. After gift opening, we would have lunch and most, led by Mom and Dad, might take a nap. Following that, we dress and assemble to drive to the neighboring Colgans.

COLGAN'S CHRISTMAS DINNER

C*hristmas dinner at* the Colgans was always great. Nanny would join us, and occasionally Grandfather Castleman. Aunt Polly's father would make it in his wheelchair (one leg had been amputated below the knee due to diabetes). We enter via the back door after crossing the large screened in back porch with day bed and table into to the kitchen with a huge coal-fired stove now used as a catch all and table. Past the fridge and before the electric stove is a walk-in pantry with sink, dishwasher and work table. Back in the kitchen, take a left in front of the coal stove and enter a small bedroom followed by a small bath. Take a left past the coal stove and enter the dining room with Christmas tree to the left past a fireplace, followed by the entry-hall, covered front concrete porch with swing and large front yard. Turning right from the entry-hall is the living room/den with couch, recliner and TV. At the end of the entry-hall, before the front yard are the steps leading upstairs to three bedrooms and two and one-half baths. The entry-hall also accommodates a small coat closet beneath the stairs, the Thanksgiving children's dining table, and a baby grand piano.

Uncle Bobby was formerly a drummer in a band and alcoholic, now a loyal AA member, expert bow-tie tier, insurance agent and sometime comic. He called me W.C. Taylor and Terry, Terrible Terry which stuck (and, as he would say, "Pal, spelled Pill." Aunt Polly, the family and resident equestrian, co-ran a rare and highly regarded publishing house for children's plays, located adjacent to Anchorage School. The family owned a red five-gaited saddle horse named Little Brother and a small, gray child's pony that coughed, farted and kicked at the same time, named G.G. It was Aunt Polly who encouraged Dad to purchase Mal Arrive, a red Tennessee Walking Horse and Pee Wee, a Welch pony, and cart. The theory was that Aunt Polly and Dad could ride the two big horses (which never happened), the children could ride the ponies when old enough and the big horses later and Aunt Polly would advise and consult on care and feeding.

VIOLA P. JONES

Early the next year, the most important and loved person after our parents and Nanny (kin) entered our lives. After a string of about three failed candidates, including a nice white woman named Cora who lasted about three weeks, we met Viola. I don't know how we found her, because women protect contact with black help more fiercely than they protect their own children. She lived with her husband and children, in a small brick house, with an outdoor water pump and outhouse, at the end of a deeply pitted dirt (and some gravel) path, about two miles across the railroad tracks in Berrytown. Despite no indoor running water, she was without a doubt the cleanest person, with the cleanest uniform and apron, you have ever seen. She was about five feet two inches tall and very well fed which is a recommendation right there. Her cooking was off the charts out of this world! Fluffy buttermilk biscuits, home smashed potatoes and fried chicken soon became the family's favorite and it began to show on all of us! Viola's cooking and fresh from the dairy heavy fat milk delivered daily will lay some LB's on you. Women in Mom's day were not usually good cooks and Mom was no exception. I guess they figured that if they learned how to cook, more would be expected of them. It seemed to work well for them, if not us.

    Viola came at midday usually in time to fix lunch. Afterwards she would spend about all afternoon chopping, peeling, pounding, scraping everything in sight, roll out the dough for cutting into biscuits, and get out all the pots and pans she would need to cook dinner. After a little dusting and light cleaning downstairs, she would usually retire to her maid's room off the back porch, maybe lie down for some brief shut-eye, then wash up and change her uniform and apron for dinner. She would then commence cooking dinner, after which she would serve up plates for whoever would be eating in the breakfast room, which was anyone under the requisite age of six, the age required to graduate into the dining room. Finally, she would ring the small silver dinner bell that stayed at the head of the table which would be rung during dinner to summon her when needed. At the sound of the bell we all came tumbling into our respective room for eating, all shirt-tails tucked in. At a full table, Mother would sit at the head near the dining room door with Terry to her right, next was me, then Dad sat at the other end. Robin was seated at Dad's right and then came Gwathmey seated at Mom's left. Terry could be reached by Mom and Robin and I within reach of Dad to be assisted or scolded as required. Both Mom and Dad came with Scotch and water in hand after spending whatever available time together, catching up on the day's news, including child report, newspaper and a Chesterfield in the den. After we were all seated, whoever's week it was would say the blessing after we bowed our heads, "Give us grateful hearts oh Lord, for these, and all thy blessings, sanctify them for our use, and save us for Christ's sake,

Amen." Mother then rang the dinner bell and Viola would appear from the kitchen, first bringing the meat and returning to the kitchen for all the vegetables, all served from silver serving dishes. After serving each family member and guest she would place the serving dishes on the sideboard, return to the kitchen, and tend to anyone eating in the breakfast room. After an appropriate time, she would return to the dining room doorway inquiring if anyone needed to have their drink re-filled or wanted seconds. About then, wanting to make sure they were leaving enough room in their stomach, someone would inquire what was for dessert, if anything, to which she would respond. After re-filling the requisite drinks, and serving any seconds requested, she would return all the serving dishes to the kitchen, and reappear once again at the doorway, asking for a show of hands from those wanting dessert. Upon getting the count, she closed the door and began serving dessert on plates in the kitchen. She then served each desert plate individually while collecting the dinner plates and returning to the kitchen to fill the dishwasher and cleaning all utensils and serving dishes by hand. When everyone finished dessert, Mother would ring the bell and Viola would reappear to collect dessert plates while everyone would request permission to leave the table, and when granted and their napkin was neatly folded at their place, would file out of the room—often to the den to see evening news or upstairs to commence homework. Upon completing clean-up, Viola would appear at the den door, saying she was ready. Mother or Dad would take whatever child requested to join them and head toward the front door, meet Viola with her brown paper bag carrying clothes, and all get in the car. On the way home everyone would moan how good the dinner was and how full they were. After dropping Viola at her door, the return to our home was a good time to make any pertinent request of the parent or conversely for the parent to quiz the child about any recently divulged misbehavior. In later years learning drivers accompanied by an adult would drive Viola home, which was particularly challenging, with the pitted path yanking the wheel from your hand as the car pitched from side to side heading for the roadside ditch. Upon arriving home and depositing passengers at the house, the chauffeur would head down the driveway onto the gravel road and park the car in the garage, walking back up to the house and repeating the task, until all three garage spaces were filled, if required.

We boys could tell Viola anything and ask her any question. Viola often responding with, "Billy, you don't really mean that," as only she could say it. Her heart was pure gold and as big as all outdoors. She would often defend us to Mother, but could scold us just as quickly. She was a true and trusted friend. As we matured, we had more questions. Why did she have to live in a house like that with no running water? Couldn't Dad pay her more money? Could we just repave the road for her? Over the years we learned a lot about economics and how much money people made and what happens if you overpaid or underpaid someone. We learned about race relations and watched it change. We asked what would happen to Viola if she got sick and couldn't work. Did she get a paid vacation? (I think when we went on vacation, so did she and Dad paid her what he could.) What would happen to her if and when she retired? How would she live then? The general answer was that she never really retired. When Mom and Dad had to move to St. Louis for Dad to find work, after he was laid off from his job just before he was to start receiving his pension (laws never change fast enough) Viola went to work for Gwathmey and other relatives. Eventually, when she was about 70 (nobody really knew how old she was) her son-in-law built her a small house with indoor bathroom and shower, right next to her old house where her son and wife and grandchildren lived. We all came home eventually and attended her funeral and cried for days. Dad respected all black people. Against the advice of most of his friends, he made a large loan to one of our favorite waiters at Owl Creek across the street. Several of his wealthier friends in the early 60's invested in the boxer Cassius Clay, the Louisville Lip. When he suddenly changed his name to Mohammed Ali and changed his religion to Muslim, they went running for the hills. As one of Dad's favorite politicians, Ronald Reagan said (whom Dad supported at the outset) "Trust but Verify". Dad did not support Lyndon Johnson, or John F. Kennedy, or the war on poverty, because critical thinking allowed him to accurately predict the outcome—which would be destruction of the black family, work ethic and jobs of the black man coupled with spiraling crime and poverty. Dad did not approve of the subsequent black riots, but did not radically oppose them either.

Dad was tough. He had to be. He had four boys to raise and educate. The critical thinking base line begins to fill, but it still has a long way to go.

With the second half of third grade starting, we were over a year into rehab. The routine was setting in. We said a blessing at every meal, and said prayers together with our roommate every night. It would start in every night after brushing our teeth. "Now I lay me down to sleep, I pray the Lord my soul to keep. If I should die before I wake, I pray the Lord my soul to take." Pretty gruesome for an eight-year-old. Early on I asked Mom what "If ahh shud da before I wake" meant and she spelled it out for me. We continued, "God bless Mom, Dad, Gwathmey, Robin, Billy and Terry, Grandmother Tyler, Nanny and Paw Paw, Uncle Bobby, Aunt Polly, Sissy, Bobby, and Marie. Susie, Sheila, Sugar and Spice." As we grew older it got more complicated with this proven cure for Alzheimer's, " God bless Coogie, Two, Gwathmey, Judy, Gwathmey, Jenny, Esme, Levi and Briggs, Davis, Marquinia, and Samuel, Colgan, Ya Ya, Carolina and Julian. Robin and Marty, Bo and Margaret, Harley, Edward, and Bo, Austin and Brooke, Renn and Levi, Molly and Gilbert, Billy and Beth, Meg, and Jeff Audrey and Eva, Will, Hayley, and Henry. Terry and Mandy, Welby, Lee Courtney, Shay, Logan, Baylor and Eloise (47)." For extra measure add in all your spouse's relatives. And you thought memorizing your catechism was hard?! Like in all good American families there were six divorces and four deaths (not counting Coogie and Two). None of the divorces and deaths were related. Just like with the four older brothers, with our annual gatherings, everyone can praise, criticize, shape, mold, envy, reject, and emulate everybody else. And if you don't think everybody isn't watching you every minute of every day, just check your messages, emails, Facebook, and other social devices a few times. As someone once said, it takes a village and ours covers four states and takes four breaths to get through! Soo...add to this at least one meal blessing a day and Sunday school followed by a service once a week except for summer break, you get a pretty good religious base for solid critical thinking. Conservative vs. liberal learning, yet to come.

GWATHMEY AND ROBIN

By this time, Robin was 10, in fifth grade and Gwathmey was 13 in ninth grade, almost ready to graduate from Anchorage School. Robin was already beginning to lay claim to the family athlete title, having abdicated the scholarship ribbon earlier. He was excelling in all the sports-basketball, soccer, baseball and football at school and across the street at Owl Creek, in swimming, tennis and golf—plus he was still hogging time at the train table. Gwathmey dabbled at basketball and swimming, but really excelled in tennis. He also still held rank as head engineer at the train table. We were all good at ping-pong. Gwathmey was beginning to show signs of a growing back problem, eventually diagnosed as Spinal bifida aculta. After graduating from Anchorage, he was fitted for a back brace which he wore through high school, a plywood board was installed under his mattress, and he was required to spend two hours lying on his stomach each afternoon. He finally grew out of it as anticipated.

LOUISVILLE COUNTRY CLUB

Mom and Dad were both members of the Louisville Country Club growing up, and likely met at a debut party there. Amenities there include an 18-hole, championship golf course, practice area, several clay tennis courts, a platform tennis/squash court, large swimming pool with high dive, beautiful three level clubhouse with public and private dining rooms, men's grill and bar, and two lavish ballrooms. Only two Anchorage families held memberships there, the Caldwells with their four boys and the Tylers with their four (Mac Caldwell, the oldest dropped dead of a heart attack on the paddle tennis court there at about 55.) When you entered the eighth grade and continuing on through the ninth you were eligible to attend Mary Long Burke's Cotillion classes in the main ballroom for five continuous weeks on Friday nights from 4:30 to 6:00 p.m. in the fall. We would rotate carpool with three other families and the only other Anchorageite I can remember was Barbara Waterfill in my class. We would shine our shoes and dress up in coat and tie, and the girls would wear fancy dresses and their first pair of low heels. We would learn the fox trot, waltz, rhumba, samba, and jitterbug, all accompanied by Henry Robbins at the piano, who later became Robin's piano teacher. We would start each dance with the girls lined up on one side of the room, and boys, always jockeying for position across from our favorite girl de jour on the other side. We would then come together, taking the correct holding position depending on the dance, each inspected and adjusted by Mrs. Burke or one of her assistants. Finally, we would morph into a circle, dancing our way around the room, stopping from time to time to correct mistakes by several couples who were mercilessly embarrassed in front of their friends. After a while we were forced to change partners and start again. From time to time there were Award Dances where a handful of silver dollars were distributed to the proud winners. I remember after receiving my award, calculating how long it would take me to earn my first million dollars by winning a dollar for each dance step (early critical thinking). I think everyone eventually won an award. We met a ton of our parents' friends' children this way who lived in town and went to different schools. Over time we would date, go to debutante parties, and maintain long term friendships. Most of the guys attended Louisville Country Day School and the girls attended Louisville Collegiate and Kentucky Home School.

Robin also became an equestrian champion. Many afternoons and in the summer, he would saddle up Pee Wee and often Marie would harness GG and off they would ride down the trails of Anchorage. Anchorage had a lot of horse riders and even more trails. Our most frequented trail ran behind our house next to the Navin's horse farm, behind the Eggers farm and exiting onto LaGrange Road. After a short stretch you turn left on Osage Road and along holes four and five at Owl Creek C.C. returning at full gallop up our driveway (Pee Wee was going home and could not be stopped) to the barn.

ST. LUKE'S FAIR AND HORSE SHOW

Every May, about the second or third Saturday, The Annual Anchorage Saint Luke's Fair and Horse Show was held on the Pat White property, just around the corner from the church. It cranked up around 9 a.m. featuring joy rides, game booths, football toss, pony rides, bakery contest booth, jams and jelly booth, dunking booth, kissing booth, screened in food porch with barbeque with all the trimmings, auction stage, and a huge horse show ring. The game booths and rides started at 9 a.m. peaking about 1 or 2 p.m. The Horse Show ran from about 12:30 to 4:30 p.m., with the auction running from about 4:30 to 6:30 p.m., competing with dinner from about 5:30 to 7:00 p.m. The Horse Show was on the regional circuit and winning points were earned for the Annual State Horse Show. The Horse Show was manned, judged and announced by professionals. As mentioned, Anchorage had plenty of riders, and the show attracted equestrians from all over the state. The rest of the fair was manned by everyone you knew in Anchorage and some you didn't know. Mom (Viola) contributed a cake to the cake sale (and purchased it back half of the time), took a turn in the kissing booth, and Dad was the Auctioneer. All proceeds went to St. Luke's Church. In the morning, Mom would purchase a number of tickets for each of us, the number varying with age. We would spend the rest of the day chasing her down to beg from some of the extras she always purchased. If we couldn't find her, we would try to hit up Dad which never worked. Then we would cruise the "mall" looking for buddies we had pre-arranged a meeting with or just head for the shortest line. Thus began our early training in money and time management. The goal was to see the most friends, have the best time, and make the money last to dinner (so you were not forced to wander around with others knowing you had neither money or friends). Which booths ate up the most time and least number of tickets? Did you really want people to see you standing in line at the kissing booth and start receiving never ending grief even if it was for the beautiful upper-class cheerleader you had had a crush on since third grade? Did you really want to spend those tickets that Mom had told you to save for dinner, or would she save you from starvation in the end? A highlight was always Dad as Auctioneer. What talent and skill?!! That was my Dad! He even made a rare appearance one year in the Dunking Booth chair-selling a record number of tickets for the privilege of viewing, just to show he too was human!

For maybe three years, Robin and Pee Wee entered the sack race! There were always too many entries, but when the music started, they slowly proceeded around the ring, mounted, passing a number of gunny sacks on the interior ring along the way. When the music stopped, you moved as fast as you could to the closest sack, dismounted, standing on the sack while maintaining a hold on the reins to your mount. They would then remove one sack and repeat. The crowd and cheers grew with each round. Toward the end approaching four sacks, mounts were running one quarter of the way around the ring, charging clockwise or counter clockwise to the closest sack. Sometimes two or three would head to one sack potentially leaving one vacant that would lead to another race. One sack left, each horse would approach the sack slowly, then gradually gain speed after passing it, to close the gap heading around to the sack again. This last round always seemed to last the longest with suspense, crowd and cheering growing every time a horse passed the sack. The music stopped. A mad dash by both participants either side by side, to avoid the delay of turning around, or from opposite directions at break-neck speeds, all depending on the speed of the mount and skill of the rider! Reaching the sack, each rider would fly through the air heading toward the sack, attempting to keep their balance and hold onto a lurching mount simultaneously—each rider landing on the sack, blocking the other to knock him off the sack and/ or make him lose control of his mount. Just like at home plate, the umpire would then dramatically identify the winner, to the uproariously loud cheers and boos of the crowd! It was always the highlight of the day!! Robin and Pee Wee finally won it their third year. A cherished blue ribbon was proudly displayed in Pee Wee's stall that night!

Back to Anchorage School for the winter and spring terms in third grade. Still pretty much of a grind. One brighter spot, I got introduced to Mrs. Hays and her library. She had silver gray hair and, unfortunately, halitosis. Her daughter Sherry was in my class and son Dennis was in Robin's class so she was friendly to us both. I took on the Dewey Decimal Filing System with a vengeance. I really started to enjoy reading. Mrs. Hall could always come up with a good suggestion at my reading level. It wasn't long before I became a library assistant, helping others find what they were looking for. I thought that learning the library filing system would be worth the effort as I moved up the education ladder, which it was until it was eventually replaced by Google as were so many other things.

THE KENTUCKY DERBY

The first Saturday in May, ever since 1875, is Kentucky Derby Day at Churchill Downs in downtown Louisville. When Mom cruised around the world with her Uncle about two years before getting married to Dad, she met Leon Mandle and his wife who lived in California and had a Derby Box for a number of years but were tired of attending. She put Dad in touch with them and they gave it to Dad every year with Dad's insistence that they stay with us if they ever attend in person. Eventually the box was given to Dad after Leon died by his wife. Subsequently, most boxes were confiscated by the track owners at the death of the holder to be purchased by large corporations which presumably would pay larger fees and bet larger sums of money, unless the owner's family successfully performed a miracle, of which we lucked into two (to be continued). Derby Weekend includes two full days of racing on both turf and dirt surfaces, +/- 10 to 12 races per day, with the feature event for Friday being the Oaks race for fillies, and the Derby for top qualifying three-year-olds run late Saturday afternoon. The race length is one and a quarter miles, typically supports the largest field of the Triple Crown (20-21 horses) and the record time is two minutes held by Secretariat. The box seats six and typically there are about 100,000 in the stands and 30-50,000 in the infield. The cost for the seats for Derby Weekend is about equal to the cost for all days of racing in the spring and fall meets combined. When we were young, Mom and Dad typically filled the box with clients with cocktail and dinner parties either at the house or Louisville Country Club. Everything was a high fashion coat and tie affair with one of a kind ladies' hats in order for Friday and Saturday. A guest friend of mine to the Derby one year proclaimed Derby Day as the best combination ever for pure pleasure. Where else can you spend the day outside, smoking a cigar, drinking fine whiskey, surrounded by beautiful women dressed to the nines, gamble and win money. Later after we became of age we took our turns in the seats, and finally included our girlfriends, wives, friends and relatives. The whole town is abuzz with parties, with one of the largest held in Anchorage between our house and the Colgans. It was hosted by property owner Anna Friedman in honor of the Kentucky Colonels (quasi political group), with tents, tables, and chairs provided by and set up by troops from nearby Fort Knox with round the clock mint juleps, barbeque, burgoo and bands. The Tyler boys, never invited, made general nuisances of ourselves, hid in the bushes and were regularly thrown out only to sneak back in.

This was the year that Robin caused perhaps the most unforgettable Derby for most of us, certainly our parents. It was Wednesday or Thursday afternoon, and our always-take-a risk, never in doubt athlete chose to swing like a chimpanzee from overhead pipes above the concrete floor in the boys' bathroom on the bottom level of Anchorage School, landing on his head with his eyes closed and blood streaming from his ears, prompting me to scream for help from everyone, including a slow ambulance which carried Robin to Norton's Infirmary. He was diagnosed with a concussion and assigned to the emergency room. Mom, uncontrollable and inconsolable, arrived at the hospital with somber and unimpressed Dad in tow. Robin, in an attempt to calm Mom, weakly asked her to come to his bedside so he could talk to her. She bent over the bed of her bandaged son, and he whispered "Bet it all on Dark Star on Saturday" whereupon she cried even louder and Dad's scowl deepened as he turned redder. Dad announced he would take care of the houseguests and attend the track on Friday and Saturday so Mom could tend Robin. Mom, confident that Robin had severe and untreatable brain damage, summoned the nurse to secure some adult beverages for her and Dad. Robin's condition improved the next day and into the weekend, and Mom almost joined Dad at the Track on Saturday, but stayed at the hospital, rethinking her betting strategy. Sure enough, Robin recovered, none the worse for wear, and you guessed it, Dark Star won that year's Derby! Mother had not bet it all, but bet plenty, and won big. Robin, always pressing his luck, claimed half the winnings.

As mentioned, Derby was always a big time for entertaining Dad's clients from out of town, many, from time to time staying at our house. I remember one year, a guest, from some big city or California asked to use the phone, to make a long-distance call to check on his family. Now, at that time, you would pick up the receiver and a voice would say "number, please," and if the call was elsewhere within Anchorage, you would recite a simple three-digit number, if Louisville, a five-digit number, if in state, but out of Louisville you would need to request an out of town operator, and if out of state, a long- distance operator all followed by whatever digits. The operator would connect the call and if completed, someone would answer. If there was no answer after a period, the operator would say "no answer" and if in use, the operator would say the line is busy. The operator would inquire if you wanted her to keep trying, you would so indicate and after a few minutes the call would be answered or the operator would request that you call back later.

Our guest, after going through several iterations and finally completing a conversation with his family, returned to the party at the house, declaring that Anchorage had the most innovative, advanced, courteous, and polite phone system in the U.S.!

The next major event in the spring comes at the end of May on Memorial Day, one and a half hours north of Louisville in Indianapolis, Indiana, ever since 1916. Dad had owned four seats on the first turn of the oval track since 1932. As said earlier, Dad loved cars a lot. He was full of information of all sorts about cars including all there is to know about Indy. As a young child he could tell you what car was coming down the street just by listening to the motor. The Kentucky Derby takes about two minutes to complete as "the two fastest minutes in sports." The Indy 500 takes about four to five hours. Of the two events, Mom said Indy was her favorite. In 2016 for the 100th running of the Indy 500, all four Tyler brothers occupied the Tyler box, as someone named Tyler had done for over 75 years.

13 ACRES

Dad must have said it a million times, sometimes with a lot more emphasis than others, "We have 13 ('penis' acres as mom referred to them) out there, now turn off the TV and get your butts out there!" He was right, by my count: there were over 20 things you could do out there, depending on age, weather, and friends. Right out the back door was a sandbox, nearby water hose for making rivers, shovels and tractors. Next to that there were two swings and a sliding board. Next to that was the playhouse housing bicycles and tricycles. One day, Robin was riding my two-wheeler down the driveway with me on the back fender. He went faster and faster. I told him three times to slow down or I would jump off. I jumped! Very poor critical thinking! As Mother drove me to the doctor with Robin holding compresses on my bleeding wounds, she shouted, "Why were you going so fast?" to which he responded, "I didn't think he would jump!" No broken bones, just scrapes and scratches everywhere. Behind the playhouse were the horse pastures, where we spent hours and days riding Pee Wee and Mal Arrive. Next to that was the garage with the requisite basketball hoop (in Kentucky, a requirement to receive an occupancy permit for a residence). The garage roof was perfect for solo pitch and catch. Next to the garage was the little efficiency cottage where Terry stored his snakes, turtles, lizards and other reptiles not requiring constant heat. Back up the driveway closer to the house were the walnut trees, which shed green walnuts the size of small baseballs and even harder. To prepare for a good fight among four or five of your bravest friends, you collect a pile of ammo and hide behind a tree and then come out hurling, receiving return fire from all directions. When you run out of ammo you need to pick up more from the ground receiving an even bigger hail of fire. Finally, someone got hit very close to an eye, which prompted a permanent cease fire enforced rigorously by a team of parents and casualty insurance men. It was great training for the military. Glad I never had to serve. The large field in front of the house was constantly in use. At the bottom of the yard was a red maple, with low branches that made it perfect for climbing. Kites were flown on windy fall days and always got caught in the trees (which Dad discouraged). Softball was popular, with a tree being used for first base, somebody's jacket normally used for second, stump near the driveway circle was third and home plate was a hubcap. Wiffle ball made for a more leisurely competition. Pitch and catch with a hardball was required to break in a new glove and warm up for school competition. Soccer was played but not popular. Croquet was played intermittently. Later, golf was the rage, with Robin hitting the long ball, and finally hitting the clubhouse across the street. We would hit a small bucket of balls toward the street with an iron, never sure how far they would go. Not wanting to waste any effort, we would then go out and hit them back toward the house, occasionally bouncing one into a car in the driveway. If Dad found out, he would fume and just shake his head. The Club had a tennis backboard which we all used from time to time. One afternoon, Terry and I headed over to practice doubles on the backboard and Sheila, the black standard poodle, followed us. All the dogs would go to the Club from time to time, getting into the garbage, prompting calls from the manager for us to come retrieve them and secure them inside. There were always golf caddies hanging around, waiting to get hired. Bored, several were just standing around watching me and Terry. I am not sure what got into me, but I decided to yell, "Sheila, sic'em, sic'em arrrarrrrarrrr." To my amazement she took after them, scattering them. She ran one up a tree, biting him squarely by the ankle. I quickly grabbed her collar and hauled her off. Terry and I checked on the caddy who was bleeding pretty good, and apologized to him as his buddies hauled him off for bandaging, cussing us loudly. Terry and I decided we had better skedaddle, and alert the parents in anticipation of the worst. Mom called Dad at work in the hopes he might calm down driving home. He was still a category five upon arrival! He was just warming up on his guilt and punishment speech, into his third "What were you thinking???"! when the phone rang. It was the caddy's parents and Dad took the receiver. He promised full cash payment for any doctor treatments, lost time at work etc. He then asked to speak to the caddy, asked about the event, pain etc. apologized, and asked him to hold, handing me the receiver. Shaking, trembling, almost in tears, I stumbled through an apology, handed him the receiver, ran upstairs to my room, slammed the door, and burst out crying. After conferring with Mother, Dad came upstairs and entered my room, still seeking an answer to "What were you thinking?" There obviously was no good answer, but I decided to pick Robin's old standby of "I didn't think she would do it" which didn't work for me either. After getting a strong verbal from me that I would never, ever, do anything that stupid again, he outlined the remainder of my punishment, quietly exited and poured a double scotch, I am sure. Dreading it, I awaited the call for dinner, during and after which I did not utter a word. Following that incident, I limited my front yard activity, to the occasional flying of a balsawood airplane, powered by a rubber band propeller, praying it would not get caught in the trees. It seemed the only and safest alternative until the storm clouds finally blew away. An unforgivable, and unforgettable failure of critical thinking!

(Next page shows the old "Tyler Anchorage Estate," which has been added on to by current owner as of 2018.)

THE ATHENAEUM LITERARY ASSOCIATION

G*wathmey graduated from* Anchorage School in June 1957, entering Eastern High School in Middletown, ten minutes from home, in August. He was immediately rushed for ALA, a Literary Fraternity founded in 1870 at Louisville Male High School for which Dad served as scribe at Male High in 1927. Gwathmey pledged, made it through initiation and Hell Week and was admitted before the end of the year. Competing Louisville High School fraternities included Dignitas, Chevalier, Sigma, and Fidalian. In addition, there were high school sororities as well. The fraternities also competed in athletics including basketball, football and softball. Each had a separately designed pin worn in the top right-hand corner of the pocket on your dress shirt. Traditionally you awarded it to the girl you were going steady with and she wore it on a chain around her neck.

Each Saturday, we would gather at Ogden's field in Louisville, belonging to an alumni family, around nine a.m., transfer into trucks, and/or rented trailers to either fell trees and cut them into firewood or go to the cooperage where whiskey barrels were made and load the scrap "off-fall" which was already cut into firewood, and return to the field to unload it before dinner. Sometimes on Sundays, weekday afternoons or the next weekend, we would deliver the wood to families who had purchased it from a member. The proceeds would be used for special parties in the fall, Christmas holidays or spring. Pledges served as slaves during these Saturday "work parties," as they were called, and required to sell, collect and distribute the firewood. They were also required to make and decorate a number of ceremonial hand paddles for each senior member, with which you were severely beaten. Pledging continued throughout the fall, culminating in Hell Week, and you received your pin and were inducted as a member at a special ceremony at the beginning of the year. The Christmas black tie or tails ball was usually held in the LLC ballroom. The dates of the seniors, or Sponsors as they were called, dressed in their finest ball gowns, would be presented under spotlight and to loud applause as they emerged from a giant replica of the ALA pin, which was considered a great honor. Everyone then whirled around the ballroom accompanied by a full dance orchestra!

Election of the officers was held twice a year, at the first of the year, for the Winter/Spring term and in May for the Fall term. The titles were Pledge Chairman (serving a full year term), Scribe, Treasurer, Vice-President and President. The meetings were held under the strict guidelines of Roberts Rules of Order, which were required reading of all members, and they were often cited and read, word-for-word to resolve parliamentary disputes in the weekly meetings. The meetings were held in the Parish Hall of St. Francis in the Fields Episcopal Church, just North and West of Louisville. Strictly at 7 p.m. every Saturday night, the meeting was gaveled to order, with late arrivals levied a heavy fine, or not allowed entry into the hall if too tardy. It began with a prayer, followed by the reading of the minutes, followed by a prescribed agenda of standing committee and special committee reports. Comments and questions were generated by raising your hand, to be acknowledged (or ignored) by the President. If a debate, or point-of-order was called, the times for presentation and rebuttal were strictly enforced. The next- to- last order of the night was senior session, at which time any senior was acknowledged (or not) by the President from a raised hand and time was unlimited. This time was used to air an item of concern, ask a special question, tell a story, tell jokes, or whatever. The last order on the agenda was to acknowledge any visiting alumni, seated on the back row, and their presentation time was also unlimited. When the meeting was adjourned, all the members formed a circle with arms joined at the shoulder, slowly swayed from side to side, and sing the solemn Athenaeum Hymn as done for generations:

Come Pledge to the Athenaeum, Our love of wine and song
The bond of high school friendship, a bond full soft yet strong

> *Now raise high and drain your glasses and fill your hearts with praise*
> *For High and The Athenaeum, and friendship's sunny days.*

All of this means you generally depart from the hall about 9:45 or 10 p.m. to retrieve your date to party, arriving home hopefully by 1 a.m. The requirements for the office of President are therefore fairness in running the meeting, strict knowledge of, and adherence to the rules, and constant awareness of the clock all governed and balanced by critical thinking. Without all of these, you lose all respect from your peers and the meetings last forever. Gwathmey served one term as Scribe and one as Vice-President, Robin served one term as Vice-President and one as President. I served one term as Vice-President, and two as President, and was finally further honored as Medal Man which had not been awarded in 15 years. Terry served as Vice-President and President.

Why high school fraternities? Why Athenaeum? Over the years the only other town I found them in was Birmingham, Alabama. Why ALA? It was founded as a real Literary Society, in a high school, and with a faculty advisor. Annually, they published their magazine, "The Spectator", a collection of essays, short stories and poems. Today, they are a social club, self- governed, with no faculty advisor, that annually publishes "The Spectator", that contains, essays, short stories and poems contributed by members, photos of the membership, photos of parties, club propaganda, history and ads to defray costs. "The Spectator" over the years served the club well as a legitimization factor, if for nothing else. The club obviously morphed over time. What purpose does it serve, what are the good, bad and ugly points? The purpose it serves today is a legitimate environment for boys to socialize and mature with other like-minded, upper income, well educated, men in a group that is approved by the members and their parents and tolerated by the schools and police—in other words it is a gang for rich, white, prep-school boys. An unusual benefit is that the membership is spread over about eight public high schools, prep schools and religious schools. These schools include: public schools—Eastern, Waggener, Westport, and Atherton; private schools—Louisville Country Day School for Boys; and Catholic schools—Catholic Country Day School, Trinity and St. Xavier. The private girls' schools that many of our dates attended were The Louisville Collegiate School, Kentucky Home, and Sacred Heart Academy. After my junior year in high school, I asked my father if I could transfer to Louisville Country

Day School since it was academically superior to Waggener and I had so many friends there. His response was sure, but I would have to give up summer camp. I chose Camp Dudley—another exercise in critical thinking, although maybe not my best. More about that later. A negative is that membership is exclusionary. Some argue it harms excluded members, causing depression. Other scholars, like my father, argued that if you have some flaws that make you unacceptable to your peers, then it is better (less harmful now) to learn it early when you might be able to do something about it, than learn about it at 35 when it would be more painful and expensive. We had one friend whose father had been a member and could not get elected year-after-year. He just tried too hard. You were not supposed to covet membership. It was just supposed to happen. He later became a very successful salesman and friend to all the members. Some have tried to argue that high school fraternities formed to exclude African-Americans. Remember, this was the early 1960s. Brown vs The Board of Education was only decided in 1954 and it took many years to implement. Anchorage Public School had no black students, nearby Eastern High School was just beginning to increase black enrollment, and at Waggener, located in a better demographic than Eastern, I only had one black in my class. One day in my senior year when I was President, someone spray painted the letters ALA on a bridge downtown. The newspaper then ran a liberal-leftist article slamming high school fraternities, suggesting an elitist and anti-racial tie, and even leaving the impression it could have been a racial protest. After it was published, I was called by the paper to comment. I was shocked. First, I stated, that no member of ALA could have been responsible, second it could have been done by a rival fraternity to harm ALA, thirdly it could have something to do with neighbor state, ALAbama (an A for creativity here). A follow-up article appeared the next day adding more fuel to the fire. Eventually it died down.

Remember this was 1965. JFK had defeated Nixon in 1960 which increased political and anti-racial dialogue. I remember watching Walter Cronkite describe The Bay of Pigs Invasion and the frightening Russian nuclear threat on a black and white TV in the Waggener gymnasium after varsity football practice in the fall. On November 22, 1963, it was announced over the Waggener public address system, that CBS news had just announced that JFK had been shot and the 3:00 pm pep rally in the gym to be held shortly thereafter to prepare for the High

School State Football Championship would be canceled. Everyone filed into the gym anyway, cheerleaders all in tears, everyone in shock. The Principal eventually called the group to order with a prayer and afterward announced that the night's game would be rescheduled and school was dismissed. All of this is to state that racial demonstrations and violence didn't really begin to materialize in Louisville until LBJ took office and the Vietnam War began to escalate the next year.

CAPE MAY ANNUALS

As would become the annual ritual, following Memorial Day, after the last day of school, we would point the old blue Station Wagon north toward Cape May come late June. Similar to last year, Dad would drop Mom, Terry and me at the Chalfonte, but this year Robin would join Gwathmey at Pasquaney and we would return to the camp at the end of the season for Water Sports, awards etc. Pasquaney was certainly a beautiful spot, but not particularly well suited to Terry's and my current condition. The famous 100 stairs (Jacob's ladder) to the water front proved to be a little tricky and strenuous on crutches. With brothers stationed at the front of us to break our fall and parents bringing up the rear to try to grab us if we slipped, Terry and I began the slow descent. Finally, at the bottom, we both about collapsed with fatigue. The water show was a little less enjoyable as we tried to regain our breath and strength and worried about the upcoming ascent. At the end of the event, we courteously waited for most of the other guests to precede us, relishing the extra rest. The ascent was even more strenuous than the descent! With our guards again stationed fore and aft, we commenced the long trudge, finally collapsing in exhaustion at the top. A long, remembered muscle building experience.

A quick tour of the Chalfonte lobby will make you feel right at home. As you enter the front Howard Street entrance through the screened door past the rocking chairs, the main desk is on the right with a swivel chair and window behind the desk and closet door to the right. In the crowded closet is a large vault facing the door with the phone and long cord on top with some files on top of that and more to the right. Guest valuables, daily desk records and cash are locked in the safe every evening. To the left of the desk mounted on the wall is a large glass-fronted, rectangular cabinet containing numbers for all the rooms, with a metal arrow mounted by each one. In each room is a buzzer mounted on the wall which when activated, points the arrow towards the number. The bellman on duty then grabs a small bucket of ice and heads to the room for more instructions: for mixers, pitcher of fresh water, more ice or help carrying luggage to the car. Upon completion, he pushes a button returning the arrow to its original position. Mounted below this room monitor is a wooden, open mail box with a deep square for each room large enough to hold mail, messages, room bills, a small daily newspaper and whatever. Below that is a rectangular marble-topped mahogany cabinet, storing mainly board games for children. On the top of the cabinet are displayed an array of daily newspapers including the "New York Times", "Philadelphia Inquirer", "Richmond Time Dispatch", "Wall Street Journal", and "USA Today." This copy is for sharing among the guests. To the left of this is a large rectangular glass enclosed sundry counter with sliding glass doors in the rear. From here the bellman dispenses stamps, candies, cigarettes, etc. making change from a cigar box on the top shelf. On the top of the counter, daily papers for purchase are located. In front of the case is a delicate Victorian sofa, with arms at each end, and to the left of the case sits a leather covered mahogany stuffed armchair, usually occupied by Henry, the stout, Senior Bellman. On the left-hand wall is a beautiful marble fireplace with an attractive wooden mantel topped by a mirror. The left opens into a card room lined with book shelves, and behind that opens into a room containing a mahogany dining room table surrounded by chairs and a mahogany sideboard and mirror. To the left are two small telephone booths that light up and are fan cooled.

Perhaps my parents' favorite friends were Jim and Wiley Wheat from Richmond, Virginia. Jim ran Wheat First Securities, which his father ran before him. Jim attended Virginia Military Institute, in Lexington, Virginia, where one afternoon while riding horseback, his eyesight finally left him. His mother was also totally blind. Wiley, his wife, read Jim's newspapers memos and letters to him daily. She was a uniquely beautiful lady, and Jim had never seen her. They generally came in August for a month, usually accompanied by Jim's mother who did beautiful crochet work, his father, son Jimmy, and a trusted sitter. The stories of Jim's activities are legendary. He would shoot geese and duck by following the sound of their wings, and on several hunts, he shot more than anyone. With a wry smile, he declared that his most feared phrase was when some hunter shouted "shoot the cripple". Jim ran for City Council in Richmond defeating two other black contenders. Bishop Gibson, pastor of the Episcopal Church the Wheats attended, rang "Three Blind Mice" from the church belfry on Election Day. Knowing the Chalfonte like the back of his hand, Jim loved to pop into Mom and Dad's bedroom unannounced as they were changing for dinner (remember, no door locks), boldly bragging, "I almost caught you this time, Claudia" as she scrambled to find a cover-up. My favorite Jim Wheat story occurred in Cape May one night in late August, when Mom, Dad, Jim and Wiley were out late in their favorite bar downtown. For the ride home, Jim decided to get some fresh air by climbing into the luggage rack on our station wagon when Mom, Wiley and Dad climbed inside. About three blocks from the bar, Dad spotted a police car in his rear-view-mirror. Just as he turned on his blue light, but not siren, Dad warned Jim and turned into a dark alley. Quickly helping Jim into the car and returning to his seat, Dad slowly moved forward just as the police rounded the corner, siren screaming. Dad stopped the car and waited for the police to approach his side of the car, obediently supplying his license and insurance card when requested. "What seems to be the problem, officer?" he inquired, receiving the response, "There is someone riding on the top of your car," whereupon Dad leaped to his feet climbing out of the car, searching everywhere. "Where?" Dad inquired, the Officer responding, "He must have climbed inside" as he shined his flashlight around the inside, on the floor and third-row seating area. Dad volunteered, "This is my wife Claudia, and friend Jim Wheat and his wife, Wiley, I think that is everyone." The officer requested Jim's license and after staring at it, said questioningly, "It says here you are blind" to which Jim responded, "That's what it is supposed to say, but, personally, I have never read it." Dad, sensing that the Officer was embarrassed and needed to be let off the hook here, offered, "Well officer, we certainly appreciate all the effort you and your partner have gone to, but I think we are done here. With your permission, we will head back to the Chalfonte where we are staying and we welcome your contacting us there if you learn anything more about this incident. Good night!"

Anne LeDuc, part owner of the Chalfonte and long-term manager, reached out to our whole Tyler family—especially to me. Never married and no children, she lived with roommate Mary Nell in a small apartment in Gramercy Park, in Manhattan. She hosted both me and Robin on our ways to camps in The City, for two days, including Statue of Liberty, United Nations Building, Empire State Building, The Ten Commandments movie, etc. She organized early summer volunteer work parties to scrape and paint all the old gingerbread and ready the hotel for the first guests that arrived at the end of June. She hired all the hotel staff, especially dining room waitresses, night watchmen, bellmen, and desk-boys, all college students. As mentioned I ran the desk for three or four years in college. As social director, she ran the Tin House cocktail parties, arranged beach parties, and was at ease with old and young alike. She was quite an athlete, coaching field hockey, soccer, tennis and golf teams at the George School in Moorestown New Jersey, which was her parents' and her ultimate home. Finally, she really helped Mom get through that first summer, finding sitters for us, giving her the histories of all incoming guests and getting her properly introduced.

Speaking of owners and managers, Calvin "Satt" Satterfield lived in Richmond with his wife Mariah and ran the Caterpillar dealership there. He owned a large sailboat, which he anchored in nearby Chesapeake Bay and every June he would sail the boat with a crew of friends up the East coast laying anchor in Cape May Marina for the rest of the summer. Mariah, their three beautiful, young daughters, Alice, Mary Minor, and little Suzi, and a sitter would drive up. Satt, being the son of owner Mini, was raised at the hotel and stood to inherit it one day (which he dreaded). Mom and Mariah became fast friends, both saddled with the young 'uns. I know Dad and Jim both enjoyed day cruises with Satt, but I never saw the yacht.

Bill and Marjory Straitor usually stayed for a month, and shared the Howard Street cottage with Artie and Fran Peter, (henceforth renamed the Straitor- Peter place). Marjory was a tall striking brunett and Bill had a great sense of humor. I don't think they had any children. The Peters had a son about Gwathmey's age that also belonged to the Athenaeum. They were both from Louisville, and although Mom and Dad seldom spent any time with them due to no real child connection, they were likely responsible for introducing us to the Chalfonte, once Mom and Dad let the word out in Louisville we were looking for a place.

Bill Lillard was a true dandy. Always dressed to the nines! Light summer slacks, neatly pressed, starched white shirt, silk summer sport coat, bright tie, two-toned shoes and a forever summer tan and smile. Middle aged not married, no kids, fawned over the old ladies and he ate it up. Every night he played bridge with them and anyone else in the card room. Then it was off to the bars till dawn. My parents liked Bill, but they were never close. You see, Bill was the first gay person I had ever known, but I didn't know it. He never let on. It was only years later, after learning about homosexuality, that I saw it. After we outgrew Cape May, and gays began being accepted, Cape May became a hotbed for gay activity as many Victorian communities did.

Tye Mudge was a great and funny old man. He and his wife came every year and would stay all summer. Every morning, after breakfast when everyone was rocking on the porch, letting breakfast digest and the beach warm up, all the kids would flock to Mr. Mudge hoping to get a sour ball from the country store in town. Mom told us not to swarm him and beg. But he liked kids and we liked him. Years later when I was working at the hotel, the young college male help would stay in the King Edward suite on the first floor at the bottom of the stairs leading to the family quarters on the second floor. The college girls, mostly waitresses, stayed in the Queen Anne Suite on the other side of the lobby leading into the dining room. The whole staff would party in the King Edward suite starting about 11-11:30 p.m. when almost everybody, except maybe the night watchman, finished work, and we would party till about 3 to 4 a.m., starting just hours later at 7 a.m. all over again. The party would start when the beer/liquor shipment arrived from the liquor store and was paid for by whomever had the best fake ID. After adding up that bill at the end of the summer, my critical thinking clicked in, and I realized I retained very little for my efforts for college beer. On many a night, Anne Le Duc would have to shut us down for general rowdiness. The worst, however, was when the King Edward door would open and ancient Mini Satterfield would enter in her ugly bathrobe with hair up in pin curlers and the rats would scatter to the shadows in the hopes of not being seen.

There was one night, however, with the party in full swing, we looked up and saw a note being lowered from a hole in the ceiling, with a message, "gather round—more coming!" Everyone gathered around while silence broke out as we all took a sip of beer and stared up at the hole. Finally, the hole opened up again as a bucket of water was poured on all with a moan ringing out. Drying off, and pouring fresh drinks, the party roar returned. In about 30 minutes, another note "Gather round." The leery crowd re-assembled, carefully spaced a few steps back from the whole—not to be fooled. In a few minutes, the Hole opened and an unopened bottle of scotch slowly descended to a chorus of "For You're a Jolly Good Fellow" ended by thunderous applause. He would deny it the next day, but those of us in reservations and old timers knew it was our old friend Ty Mudge!

The second summer we really got to know Cape May and what fun it could be. We hugged old acquaintances and they us, declaring how we had grown. Our physical condition had improved markedly. We could even walk to the beach carrying our sturdy canvas rafts for advanced surfing. We had conquered body surfing and by the end of the summer we were challenging the waves on our knees atop our rafts. We rented bikes, several times, riding the full length of the Boardwalk. We also were becoming expert negotiators with our parents for cash to do all sorts of activities. The miniature golf course was a constant temptation being located at the end of the sidewalk before crossing the road to the Boardwalk. The first attraction on the Boardwalk after crossing the street was the Ski-ball Arcade—an excellent opportunity to teach youth the benefits of patience, saving and skill. Each time you put your coin in the slot for a new game, the machine would belch out coupons not only just for playing, but belching even more depending on your ending score. When your coins ran out, then came the big critical thinking decisions. Do you (1) cash in now for a tiny prize or a candy bar, or (2) save your coupons to pay for more games, or (3) save your coupons for a bigger prize or (4) a combination of all the above? Just behind the cash-in counter, all the valued prizes and their cost in coupons were displayed. What could your goal be? How many coupons could you earn during the entire summer? Talk about pressure!! When it finally became your turn to decide, your brothers were yelling for you to cash it all in now, your parents were reminding you to save for future rounds, and as you were just staring at your favorite prize, everybody else in the arcade was yelling for you to just make a damn decision and get out of the way! Later you learn, life doesn't get any easier from here.

Further down the Boardwalk are Morrow's Famous Nut Shop offering every available nut on earth, and the ever-turning salt water taffy pulling machine. Even more choices including fast food, corn dogs, and seafood were still further down.

Especially on rainy days, there were the movie theater, country store with their barrels full of candy, and bowl of warm wax—you dip your finger in each year to see how they grow— the bumper cars, the merry-go-round and the list goes on and on.

As usual, Labor Day comes way too early and it is back to Anchorage School. This year it is Miss Mitchell's (Ventrice) Fourth Grade, famous for its fun arts and crafts. My big project was a paper-mache Irish Setter, about three feet long and two feet high, complete with a red yarn coat. An additional treat for me was the beginning of my trip through Scouting. Mom was a Den Mother (as if she didn't have enough to do already) and the meetings were Wednesday afternoons after school at our house. I worked my way up through the ranks of Cub, Bear, Wolf, and Webalos on to Boy Scouting starting at Tenderfoot, then First Class, Second Class, Life and then Eagle. I burned out at half way through First Class but I did make Order of The Arrow, The God and Country Medal and Platoon Leader. Gwathmey and Robin both achieved Eagle before me. I think Terry also made it to First Class. I quit just about the time of The Fumes—car fumes and perfumes—and Athenaeum pledgeship. Eight years of Scouting including two two-week stints at Scout Camp at local Covered Bridge Campground was plenty and I learned a lot.

I learned about another unique offering at Anchorage School that Fall. It was the adults-only annual musical production of the Mummers and Minstrels. Anchorage adults wrote the show, wrote the music, played in the band, designed and printed the program, acted, danced, did all the scenery and technical work, staged the show in the school theater, sold the tickets and gave all the proceeds to the school. Mom sang and danced (not her highest talent), Uncle Bob Colgan played the drums, Mr. Pendleton played electric guitar, Dad had a couple of short lines because he traveled so much, Mavis McGee who lived in a house located behind our garage on Dogwood Lane did the choreography, Liz Hogue wrote the songs, and Aunt Polly Colgan designed and printed the Play Bill. This year's show was titled "The Most Unspotted Lilly" (Shakespeare) and was a spoof centered around The Anchorage Women's Garden Club. Nothing will make you laugh harder than watching adults make fun and fools of themselves. It was a roaring success with a new show and cast every year. My first lesson in never take yourself too seriously.

The next two summers were repeats of 1956, but more fun as our health improved. Gwathmey and Robin loved Pasquaney, with Gwathmey excelling in tennis and Robin excelling in everything. The next summer, we decided to shake things up a little. Our old friend Bill McCutcheon up in Montclair, New Jersey, had been talking to Dad, about a camp that he attended as a boy, and his two sons had attended the past two years called Camp Dudley on Lake Champlain in upper state New York in Westport. It was the oldest boys camp in the country and had over 300 campers. It had hiking, camping, and water sports like Pasquaney, but lots of other sports as well, such as lacrosse, baseball, soccer, football and others. It was also on flatter land. Bill and his oldest son had visited with us at Cape May for a couple of days the summer before, talking up the camp and showing pictures to both Robin and me. Over the winter Dad either payed Robin a bribe or somehow talked him into finally doing something nice for his baby brother, but it was decided that Robin would attend Dudley the next summer to see if it was a good place for me, and maybe Terry, to attend. What a sacrifice!! So, Robin flew to Montclair to join the McCutcheons and attended Camp Dudley, while Gwathmey went back to Pasquaney, and Mom, Dad, Terry and I did Cape May. As you might expect Robin blew the doors off Camp Dudley and had a fabulous time! At the end of this summer, Mom, Dad, Terry, and I attended end of season events and awards at Dudley, leaving Gwathmey to go it alone at Pasquaney for a change. And the following summer, I was off to Dudley.

So, I spent 1961 in eighth grade at Anchorage and at Dudley, 1962 in ninth grade at Anchorage, and 1963 in tenth grade at Waggener High School and in Germany for four weeks as a Dudley exchange camper. Dudley had started the program the year before and I got a complete download from the excited returning inaugural team. I told Dad about the opportunity, promised to take German as my high school foreign language, and applied for acceptance to the program. I was accepted and despite the added tuition, Dad approved with one proviso. The previous year's group crossed over The Berlin Wall at Check Point Charlie for a visit into Communist East Berlin for an afternoon tour. The Wall had only been erected the year before, there was unrest in the city, and the specter of being put in jail in East Berlin as political prisoner held for ransom and publicity was looming. Dad said I could not go with the group into East Berlin, if they went next year. I agreed with the thought that surely relations would improve in a year, Dudley would not take an inappropriate risk, and what could Dad do to stop me that far away if I did go. The schedule was to fly to London for a few days of sightseeing, then on to Paris for more of the same. After that, we would join our German Camp Counselor guide on a bus into Germany. To get to Berlin in those days, you must first enter into East Germany. This border was under heavy guard by uniformed German Vopo soldiers armed with assault rifles, to make sure that no East Germans escaped. Our guide informed us that our bus would be inspected both outside and within by these armed guards, we should remain quiet, and obey all their requests. This was really a very active crossing and citizens were routinely shot from the guard towers attempting to leave with their families. We actually saw a family try to make a run for it across a clearing and heard shots. We doubted they would make it. You could hear a pin drop on the bus all afternoon, until we crossed out of East Germany into the West German side of Berlin. The following day we toured West Berlin and saw lots of modern redevelopment after WWII, some of which was Western propaganda to show our strength to the East Germans. The next morning, we went to Check Point Charlie, once again to be inspected by an armed militia. One of the guards stayed on our bus to insure we stayed on the prescribed route and saw only what they wanted us to see. Despite a valiant attempt to show us new development and prosperity, it was evident that this was the poor side of town. After successfully exiting East Berlin at Check Point Charlie and bidding farewell to our East German guide, our West German Camp guide pointed out the message making its way across the lighted, "Times Square" message board high in the air above the check point. It was heralding the visit by former Vice- President Richard M. Nixon into East Berlin today and expected re-entry into the West near midnight that night. For now, a little more touring of West Berlin, an early dinner at our Youth Hostel, with "lights out" at 9 p.m. to rest up for our final bus ride tomorrow to our boy's camp in Hanover for two final weeks.

RICHARD M. NIXON LIGHTS MY REPUBLICAN FLAME

Y*ou can only expect a group* of 15 to 17 year old boys away from their parents confined in a bus to stay out of trouble for just so long. A couple of my seat mates started talking about wanting to meet Nixon and sneaking out of the Youth Hostel later. I told them I was game and wanted in. We decided we would discuss the final plan, timing, and team members at dinner. Once again calling on my critical thinking skills, I came to the risky conclusion, that after disobeying Dad's visitation mandate earlier in the day, how much more trouble could I really get into by getting caught, and being sent home early with now two criminal felonies on my permanent record. C'est La Vie! The escape route was chosen, the time was set, and I was in. The plan was for four of us to exit after evening vespers around 9:30, and reconnoiter just outside the front gate and count heads. Three of us showed up and the chicken fourth was considerate enough to tell one of the others of his decision. Off to find a cab to CPC. We arrived there by 10 pm. "'A little slow tonight" was the verdict of one of the guards. We inquired as to the odds of Nixon showing up early and they responded they hoped so, but warned the last possible crossing was midnight. We waited and enjoyed a cordial conversation with the guards and a cup of coffee. About 11:50 pm as the guards went about closing up, a long, black, chauffeured limousine rambled up. After showing proper papers, they were allowed across, drove up to the three of us, and Nixon motioned us to hop in the back. He was in the front so there was plenty of room for us. They pulled off the road so as to not block any future traffic and Nixon asked for our names, home town, and the nature of our visit to Berlin. We in turn asked his and he admitted to having some dinner with some friends, and playing the piano for over an hour in the bar. He was in a jovial, chatty mood. He had just lost the election for the Presidency to John F. Kennedy and we inquired as to what was next. He said he was just making a little money for a while practicing law at his New York law firm and would see which way the wind blows. The following November 22 (my mother's birthday), Kennedy would be shot to death in Dallas, Texas. After a few more naïve questions, we asked if we could have his autograph, he happily obliged, signing three of his new business cards. Promising that we would vote for him if he ever ran again, we all shook his hand, exited, waved farewell, and happily hailed a return cab. We drew straws on the way back, with the loser given the task of hunting down a leader upon our return to admit our sins, beg forgiveness, and set up a punishment meeting for the morning. They were mostly glad we were safe, glad we checked back in to stop the worry, and even admitted to a little jealousy for our successful summit! We all pledged eternal allegiance to them the next morning and nothing further was said. Simply said, Dick Nixon lit my Republican flame. I was loyal to him until the day he died, and most likely will die a Republican conservative. And Dad even forgave me for disobeying the Supreme Command by going into East Berlin, just happy to have another conservative Republican in the house.

John Colgan is born

1840

William Colgan (PawPaw) and Claudia Tilford (Nanny) Marry June 1st

1909

John Colgan was born on December 18, 1840 and died February 1, 1916.

Colgan opened the first drugstore in 1859.

Colgan invented flavored chewing gum in 1880.

Aristides wins the first Kentucky Derby.

1850   1875   1900

Henry C and Elizabeth Colgan May 10th

1909

Samuel Gwathmey Tyler born May 28th

1912

1915

Claudia Colgan Tyler born November 22nd

William Colgan Tyler born June 10th

#1

Samuel Gwathmey Tyler III born July 2nd

#3

1942

1947

Lura Amanda Ford born January 8th.

1925

1950

Samuel Tyler and Claudia Colgan married on October 30th

1937

1945

1950

Terry Welby Tyler born May 5th

#2

Arthur Robinson Tyler born June 14th

#4

Family to Cape May—Gwathmey to Pasquany July 1st

Billy works at Chalfon—enters W&L-Ter at Pasquany—Bil pledges Beta Theta

1954

POLIO
September 15th

1958

1965

Family to Cape May—Gwathmey to Pasquany July 1st.
Billy at Dudley—Robin at Pasquany—Gwathmey attends W&L—Gwathmey pledges SAE July 1st.

Billy at Dudley German exchange—Robin enters Guilford—Terry at Pasquany July 1st.

1955

1965

1955

1966

1960

Family goes to Cape May, July 1st

Billy works at Chalfon and Guest Ty Mudge lowers whiskey throug the ceiling July 1st

PeeWee the Pony retires from pulling meat wagon around Louisville September 1st

Gwathmey goes to work in insurance agency July 2nd

Robin graduates Guilford, joins US Navy, duty in Vietnam on the USS Wainwright (1969-1971) July 1st

Robin Tyler/ Martha Austin (Marti) marry, Durham, N. C. July 15th

1972

1968

1972

SGT II, CCT, Nanny leave Anchorage for St. Louis, Mo. find work. Terry graduates Wagner High enters W&L pledges Beta June 1st.

Bill graduates W&L works in Development Office July 1st.

Shay Allen Shearer born February 21st.

Bill goes for EMORY U MBA in Atlanta lives with Gil Burke, Bob Steele of Emory med school July 1st.

1970

Gwathmey marries Nina Jefferson Davis Marret (Nina) from Smithfield, KY April 8th

Samuel Gwathmey Tyler IV born— Gwathmey/Nina April 14th

Davis Marret Tyler born September 15th

1966

1969

1972

#5

#6

#7

1974

Christopher Colgan Tyler born July 31st

Terry Welby Tyler Jr. born February 15th

#8

1975

Lee Emerson Tyler born February 18

#10

1976

SGT II, CCT, Nanny return to Louisville, works at Banner Paint Co. July 1st.

Terry graduates W&L, moves to Memphis, enters Memphis State Law, works at 1st National Bank, marries Karen Kawel Jones of Jackson, TN. July 1st.

Tyler brothers host SGT II 65th Birthday at Barney's Ball Lake Lodge, Beth and Coogie also attend July 1 Karen Tyler files for divorce July 1st.

1975

1975

1975

1976

Arthur Robinson Tyler Jr. (Bo) born June 1st

#9

Terry, Karen, Welby, Lee move to Louisville Terry attends U of L Law school, Karen goes to U of L Dental School July 1st

Bill marries Margaret Elizabeth Sherer (Beth) October 30

Courtney Elizabeth Tyler
born January 24th

Terry Tyler marries
Amanda Foard
June 6th

Claudia Marie Tyler
(Molly) born
November 6th

#11

1981

#14

1977

1981

Bill and Beth go to Paris, London, Kirkcudbrightshire, and Cumston to meet the Maitland family July 15th.

1980

1977

1980

1983

William Austin Tyler
born July 11th

#12

#13

#15

Margaret Moffatt Tyler
born January 22nd

William Colgan
Tyler Jr. born
March 30th

Samuel Gwathmey Tyler Jr. (Two) dies October 2nd

Nina Marret Tyler died December 15th

#16 #1
Esme MacDona[ld]
Tyler born | L[...]
Tyler bo[rn]

1985 **1995** **1998** **199[9]**

Claudia Colgan Tyler (Coogie) dies April 10th.

TRT Wrightsville Beach June 1st.

TRT Atlanta Olympics August 1st.

TRT vacation.

Gwathmey Tyler IV marries Heather Kleisner November 28th. TRT Frippe Island June 1st.

Tyler Reunion Trust (TRT) formed July 1st.

1985 1995

1994

Colgan Tyler adopted Alejandro Gutierrez Zúñiga September 17th

Terry Welby Tyler, Jr. died June 4th

1996

1999

TRT Tyler/ Maitland Reunion, Kirkcudbright Scotland July 1st

Ray Allen Shearer married Courtney Tyler May 11th

Meg Tyler/ Jeff Foster Wedding, Atlanta June 5th

2006

2002

2004

TRT Bo Tyler/ Margaret Bass Wedding, Nashville —Bill & Beth tour Italy for 20th wedding anniversary June 1st

TRT Wrightsville Beach, June 1st (2000 - 2005).

TRT Wrightsville Beach, June 1st (2007 - 2010).

2000

2005

Logan Welby Shearer April 3rd

2001

TRT Wrightsville Beach plus a stop in Cape May to visit Anne LeDuc June 1st

2003

2008

Austin Tyler marries Brooke Bergdahl March 15th

Audrey Elizabeth Foster born August 18th

2008 #19

Harley Robinson Tyler born June 19th

#21

2010

Eva Joyce Foster born March 31st

#23

2011

Gwathmey Tyler III marries Judith Osterman Schultze November 10th.

Gwathmey Tyler IV marries Mary Virginia Tyrell (Ginny) September 26th at Black Acre Farms settled by Edward Tyler in 1795.

Colgan Tyler marries Iyali Zúñiga (YaYa) September 25th.

2010

2009

2011 **201**

Baylor George Shearer born February 11th

#20

2011

Eloise Tyler Shearer born March 18th

#22

#2

#26

Ren Marie Tyler bo April 25th | Levi Al Tyler born March 15

John Tilley Tyler born June 16th

Lucas Jefferson Tyler born March 9th

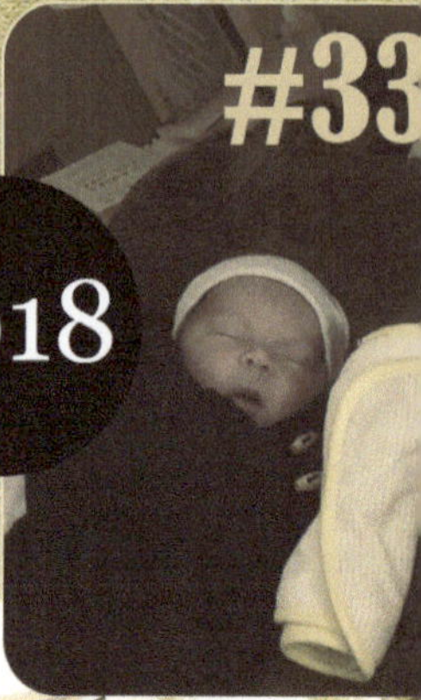

#33

2018

#30

2015

TRT Molly Tyler/ Gilbert Johnston Wedding, Linville, N.C. June 1st

2017

TRT High Hampton N.C. June 1st, 18 month old Sophie arrives November 15th.

2018

2015

2016

2017

Davis Tyler marries Marquenia Ruiz June 20th. Samuel Ruiz Tyler born September 18th.

#31

#32

Henry Colgan Tyler born March 15th

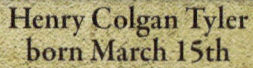

HUMOR

Having turned 16 just before leaving for camp and Germany, I was eager to start driving to Waggener. But let's back up for just a moment to add a couple of maturity achievements. Terry and I both continued to make great progress in our athletic ability which gave us more and more confidence. When not in camp in the summers of my fifth, sixth, and seventh grade years I would call up Marie and we would catch, bridle and saddle up Pee Wee and Little Brother and ride for hours on the Anchorage riding trails. Before long, we quit using the phone and would just yell EEE-AHH-KEE out the back and upon hearing a return EEE-Ahh-KEE, would saddle our mounts and meet each other half way. We even started riding bareback, Indian Style, too lazy for a saddle. Talk about building up your leg muscles! At a trot, it is damn hard not to fall off, but at a cantor or even faster gallop, it is much easier. In my seventh grade year, Gwathmey, perhaps to earn a Scout Merit badge, rebuilt the old meat wagon Pee Wee once pulled around Louisville. By mid- summer, Aunt Polly had pieced together the old harness to the Wagon and we hitched old Pee Wee up for our first ride around town which included about five of us. Pee Wee dropped about 20 years off his age and pranced around like the old days. Unfortunately, about the only place you could take the wagon was on the streets, mostly at a walk or slow trot which quickly became boring. Toward the end of the summer Marie and I found the answer. We would take the streets past the golf course, then up the slate driveway towards the Reynolds' (tobacco) Estate. Before you get to the house you get to their wide, open Polo Field. Starting at the far end you can get Pee Wee up to a full head strong cantor and maybe get him to stop before you got back to the driveway. Traveling at that speed in a buckboard across a bumpy field is the wildest amusement park ride ever invented. Unfortunately, this thrilling event came screeching to a halt on the second trip when Marie, galloping alongside the wagon on Little Brother, could not bring the big horse to a halt before the driveway, and as he hit the slippery and slightly wet slate his metal shoes slid out from under him falling on Marie's ankle which twisted and scraped on the road. We caught Little Brother, tethered his rein to the wagon, loaded Marie into the back and headed home as fast as we could. It took about two to three months on crutches for Marie to heal. That home today is owned by Papa John, the pizza king!

Having achieved this new level of physical and mental confidence, I turned subconsciously to gaining more and stronger relationships. As once described by comedian Bob Newhart, I found myself particularly at school, in small group conversations where I would make a funny or witty comment, bringing laughter to most that could hear and a "what did you say" from those out of earshot. I would then repeat the remark more loudly, and often, a larger group would laugh. This would be fine, until the teacher heard something and would ask if I would share it with the class. The best and usual response from me was to mumble my way through an apology. Sometimes I would take the broader risk and repeat my humor, usually earning me a trip to meet the Principal. If on the rare occasion that the broader group laughed and no one was visually offended, maybe even the teacher might laugh and I would get away with it. This leads me to state one of my major axioms of critical thinking which is that humorous people are not smarter than others as some profess, they are just faster thinkers. First, to be funny, you have to know what is funny to your audience. The bigger the audience, the less likely there will be a consensus, and more likely someone will be offended. All of this must be decided in milliseconds and one must have a very broad knowledge of what is most likely humorous to whom, and why. The more experience and deeper the knowledge pool the more likely the success. One way to deepen your knowledge is to broaden your repertoire. I learned to do voice impressions of Jimmy Stewart, Andy Griffith, James Cagney, JFK, Richard M. Nixon, John Wayne, Cary Grant, Clark Gable. I learned geographical dialects—German, French, British, Scottish, hillbilly, Southern, Southern black, Boston, New York City, Richmond, Virginia, and an old man. The broader the type of humor, the more likely you are to recover from a miss with a hit, in other words, not everyone likes the same joke, so give them all you've got. The funnier friends think you are and the more friends that think you are funny, the more business you get. Later I began rewriting Christmas Carols for a company Christmas party, lengthy rhyming wedding toasts, birthday toasts, special occasion toasts, you name it. But the hardest thing of all is humor on demand. I'll be honest, it all takes plenty of time.

A STRATEGIC CRITICAL THINKING EXAMPLE

The riskier the humor, sometimes the better it can be. But when you miss, it can be costly. I spent my business career providing financing for commercial real estate—apartments, office buildings, industrial, retail, and multi- use. I had a very good client I had done several deals with who needed a joint venture partner to finance the development of a multi-phase office project. Aetna, whom we represented was in that sector, so the two partners and I flew to Hartford, Aetna's headquarters, for dinner and meetings the next morning with several of Aetna's top underwriters. Dinner was at a restaurant in a downtown mall owned by Aetna. Dinner was great, we liked them, they liked us, I got a few laughs and nobody told a dead or off-color joke. This all occurred while being serenaded by a talented flautist. The Aetna guys begged off after dinner to get home to the wife and kids, while I talked the developer partners into joining me and the flautist at a bar she recommended across the street. One drink led to another and before you know it, it was 1 a.m. and a light bulb goes flashing in my head. I asked the flautist to join us for the morning presentation! The developers looked surprised and doubtful, she accepted, and I gave her the name of our hotel where we would meet for breakfast, go over the plan, and walk to Aetna's offices. At 2 a.m., I call the desk to give me a 6:30 a.m. wake-up call. OUCH! What did I do last night? Would she show? What if she didn't show? What would Aetna think? Would I get fired? I walked into the restaurant at 8 a.m., showered, shined, but hung over, having had only four and a half hours of sleep with a tough, demanding, risk filled day on stage ahead. In she walked with flute, stand and music. The developers arrived, we went over the plan, ate breakfast, and walked into Aetna's offices. I asked the receptionist to lead us to our conference room after we ordered our coffee. "Is she with you? she asked leading us. I responded with a shaky "Yes." As the flautist set up her music stand and music, I paid her our agreed-to price plus a tip. The music began as workers began filing into work. Several poked their heads in the door to confirm what they were hearing and moved on. Finally, our host from the prior evening appeared, even smiling I think, saying that we would be joined by a host of others, some who would be delayed by kids-to-school traffic, while others were trying to clear their calendars since they had just been invited to join our group. Finally, we were all assembled, the flautist folded her stand and disappeared as the preliminaries began. Our host thanked us all for coming and for the excellent entertainment (not fired yet), introduced their players and turned the floor over to me. I thanked last night's team for spending the evening with us, introduced my clients, the agenda we had planned, and took my seat. The presentation went smoothly, Aetna looked engaged, asked lots of questions, ordered more coffee, took a bathroom break, when I cornered the developers, "What do you think?" They responded with a thumbs-up gesture, a few more agenda presentation items and we agreed to ask for the order. After we reconvened and finished our summary points we asked for Aetna's thoughts. They responded in the affirmative, said that they wanted to put their heads together as to when committees meet and they could get their paperwork together, announced the caterers should be arriving any minute with lunch and each team began to huddle, and some headed for the phones. As the caterers filed in, our host asked if I could spare some time after lunch to meet with a few committee members who could not attend the morning meeting, to which I responded in the affirmative. Lunch was cordial, still more huddles and a few more questions from Aetna. Finally, Aetna summed things up by stating that they were very impressed with the presentations and the ball was in their court, heads nodding agreement around the room. They added they could meet the developers' timetable by preparing an executable application within 10 days and full committee approval and written commitment two weeks after that. Sweet success! Meeting adjourned, the developers headed to the phones, the receptionist arranged for a cab to take us to the airport and I headed off around the hall to meet with my additional committee members and one V.P. I had spoken to several times on the phone, but never met. Both committee members were cordial and confirmed that they had heard good things (and sounds) from the morning meeting, and that their personal travel schedules did not conflict with the timely committee approvals. I gave them my card and asked them to call me directly if they had any questions along the way, and I scooted to my final meeting. "So, you are flute man?"! my VP friend grinned as he stood to greet me, already knowing the answer. He confirmed the same things the others had said and we then talked backgrounds and family growth. He promised to get back to me with any behind the scenes intelligence he gleaned, and we both promised to keep in better touch with each other. We are still friends today and almost did a few deals along the way. Finally, off to the airport with two very happy borrower/developers. The deal, developers and Aetna all made money on a very successful development. The postmortem is simply this. This was a very high stakes poker game. On the table were a 75- year relationship between my company and Aetna, the careers and financial future of two developers, and my career, reputation, and future employment. I had to call on strategic critical decision-making criteria for every card that was played, from hiring a flautist to orchestrating a successful presentation and deal negotiation. In the end, what I gave these people was not a humorist, clown, or friend but a leader who could take a risk and deliver success. It was all worth it and I am thankful I had developed the critical thinking skills up to the task.

Now back to maturity development! When I was in the seventh grade and Terry the fourth, Gwathmey and Robin were invited over to a friend's house to play basketball. Their friend had a little brother my age who surely would play, so I insisted on joining. When Mother nixed it, I was furious, packed a sandwich and a jacket, decided to run away from home and talked Terry into joining me. We headed out the back door to the horse pasture and almost to the Naven's property. About then Mother came out shouting our names with blood hounds in tow. Terry said he was giving up and going back. Just after swearing he would not tell where I was hiding, he started heading back yelling "Here I come," with Mother responding, "I see you, where is Billy?" to which he answered "right here." Within three minutes I was surrounded by four tail wagging dogs. I marched home even angrier and shut myself in my room. About time for dinner,

Dad arrived in my room with the "if you were really as mature as you thought you were, you would not have run away in the first place speech." Even angrier at myself, I suffered through dinner and sulked off to bed. Chalk that up to bad critical thinking!

GO CARTS

I *am not sure whether* Dad just felt like Terry and I were due a break, or just had a break in his schedule, or what, but he decided to work with Terry and me to build us each go carts, which we were both very grateful he did. The bodies were cut out of 4x8 two-inch plywood, the axels and wheels were mounted on 2x4's. Ropes were tied to each end of the front axle, and were then wrapped around a broom stick steering shaft with a steering wheel attached. A gasoline lawn mower engine was bolted above the rear axle and a pully attached to the engine drive shaft was attached via a fan belt to a pully attached to the left rear wheel. A hand operated clutch mounted to the right of the driver, engaged the two pulleys. To the left of the driver, a hand brake was mounted that, when pulled back, pressed onto the left rear wheel. We learned all about power saws, drills, socket wrenches, shopping at Peterson's Hardware, gas engines, and most of all we learned a lot about Dad. He is patient, thorough, creative, thoughtful, funny, and all of this with no training from a Dad of his own! We raced those cars around the circle, up and down the driveway, across the yard to the subdivision and back. And only one small mishap. Robin was driving my cart up the driveway with me standing next to the engine on the back. When he pulled to a stop in front of the house, I lost may balance and my right (good) leg fell toward the engine flywheel. I then fell backward onto the driveway and saw my leg. It looked like the inside of a biology book! We called the never-speedy Anchorage Police and they drove me and Robin to Dr. Simon's office in nearby Middletown, at the Anchorage speed limit of 25 mph with Robin reminding them to hurry up before I bled to death or infection set in. With 135 stitches and lots of gauze and bandages, I was walking out of there on a new rented set of crutches. Good as new in about four weeks AND only bled four drops of blood.

ANCHORAGE TELEPHONE AND TELEGRAPH

It was about this time that I became good friends with Johnny Clark. He lived next to Anchorage School and his mother had been an early responder. She even took the health risk to bring Johnny along to see us way back then. He had an older sister Craig, Robin's age, and a younger brother, Phillip. Johnny came over to ride carts with Terry and me and was one of my first spend-the-night friends. Johnny, and an older Anchorage friend and neighbor, Lee Rupley, started our own AT&T. Lee had gone to an old Army Surplus store and purchased some old Army field telephones, two operator switchboards and plenty of wire. Then they wired up about a dozen users. I am not sure who did all the pole and tree climbing, but it took less time than I thought it would. Lee kept one switchboard and Johnny the other. All anybody had to do was crank their hand set which would buzz on both switchboards, then Johnny or Lee would connect them to the person they were calling. As you might guess, this can continue well into the night, so I was spending more and more nights at Johnny's. I lived too far away and they would somehow have to cross over the railroad tracks with wire to allow me a connection. Eventually the thrill wore off and life returned to some level of normalcy.

For some unexplained reason, I needed to try my hand at selling something and my chosen product was Amway Products. It seemed like they distributed everything under the sun, but their most popular product was laundry detergent. I made a long list of all my parents' friends and all of my friends' parents and practiced my sales pitch. Luckily, one of my first sales was to a large family, who bought the largest container of detergent Amway made and three months later reordered the same amount. They became my biggest supporter which led to my early recognition by Amway as a super-salesman. I followed this up with the sale, of all things, of horse detergent to a friend who owned three horses. I didn't even know Amway made the product, but my buyer saw it in the Amway catalogue I had left with him. I ordered more catalogues and called more customers. The company wanted me to write up the secret of my success. Critical thinking again! To make a long story short, I was hooked on commission, pyramid selling. I signed Terry up and my pyramid began. When my time with ALA began, my selling began to peter out and it was over when I left for college.

MORE TYLER BROTHER TRADITIONS

E*verybody has traditions,* but we seemed to have a lot and most were very different from those of most of our friends. This in part is because of where we lived, but also because of our parents' connections and traditions. We have already covered the Kentucky Derby and Indianapolis 500. I will cover three more here and add even more later.

Dad's mother, Edmonia, had a sister, Marguerite Blackley in Memphis, who had two sons, Norman and Winston. Norman was about Dad's age and they spent a fair amount of time together growing up. Winston who was younger spent about a year living in our back cottage, losing about four jobs and then returning to Memphis (Dad took advantage of this opportunity by lecturing us on the importance of keeping a job). Norman however was someone very special. He never married and lived in his mother's house until she died. He acquired a beautiful old mahogany Chris-Craft two- seater runabout, restored it to mint condition, and toured it around the Southeast, winning many awards in antique boat shows. He had about five recent antique automobiles partially restored in a garage behind his house. He raised, fed, clothed, and educated, more than 100 orphaned boys, eventually winning a Lion's Club special proclamation for his labor of love. He is still going at 92 today. He and Winston are on speaking terms but, unfortunately, are not close. One year, Norman showed up at our house to escort a houseboat hull he had designed and ordered, just north of us in Indiana, back to Memphis. He then built and installed two engines, and the entire interior of the boat. He christened it "The Norwin" and launched her in the Mississippi River.

Now the Mississippi River houseboats and harbor fueling stations are about the same as Interstate highways, big rig trucks, and truck stops. And houseboat captains and truck drivers have the same habits. They both go on long hauls, know lots of people along the way, and stay in constant communication, knowing generally who is traveling the same route as they are so they can help one another. None of my friends know either a big rig driver or a riverboat captain, and therefore cannot experience this sort of travel phenomenon. But we knew Norman, and every Tyler brother went on at least one five- day long boat trip, and most of us spent a couple of days on another trip. My big trip came when I was about 14. The Mississippi River is everything they say it is—fast, treacherous, ever changing currents, full of invisible sandbars, submerged logs, and lots of tugboats pushing long strings of barges. The first day you have lots to learn—port, starboard, two- way radio, sonar, wheel, throttle, rudder. The wheel is easy, but to watch where you are going, change throttle, watch the sonar and talk on the radio and can be impossible at times. Norman patiently teaches you each, emphasizing the dangers of not performing each correctly, then adding in another function. Eventually, you get comfortable with it, and Norman is confident in you, then disappears for two hours to fix a bilge pump, tinker with the engine, or fix lunch. Don't be afraid to yell, "Norman, you had better get up here quick and take a look at this…Norman, hurry!"

Early in the morning on the third day, we had just finished breakfast. We had turned into the Arkansas River late the day before and would be on it all day today. Much less barge traffic, slower current, much more serene. It was a bright, sunny, cloudless sky; I was behind the wheel; plenty of deep water judging by the sonar; very little radio chatter. Suddenly out of my left eye, I spotted him—a majestic bald eagle, king of the sky! He swooped down right in front of the boat, retrieved a handsome fish and disappeared off into the horizon. Absolutely breathtaking! Care to guess the single largest killer of bald eagles? Fish! The eagle cannot release his grip on his prey until he sets it down. True. Didn't know that did you? It can win you a drink at the bar. Now you also know why the riverboat trip with Norman is a favorite Tyler Boy tradition.

The next tradition occurred in March in Louisville Freedom Hall in '58, '59,

'62, '63, '67, '69. Still does every year, just not in Louisville. Freedom Hall seats 18,700 with the second largest venue seating only 13,000. The event is the NCAA National Basketball Final Four Tournament. In the day, the big teams were Kentucky, Indiana, Cincinnati, UCLA and others. Every year Mr. Kentucky and Mr. Indiana High School Basketball Seniors were crowned. Millions of fans live within a day's drive of Louisville. This was the center of basketball in America. Every year, Dad got plenty of tickets for his clients. You couldn't be sure what teams would be playing until the week before. That meant that Dad may go through four, five, maybe six invitations to clients to attend one of the games. The Tyler Brothers were always waiting in the wings to take their shot. Another perennial contender in those days was neighbor, Ohio State. One of Dad's major clients and one of our favorites was Vic Bazler, from Columbus, Ohio. Several years Vic, his wife Dottie, and their beautiful daughter Penny, who attended Ohio State would come and spend the weekend or longer, depending on their winning streak, at our house. Mine wasn't the only Tyler heart stolen at the end of the week by Penny. Each of the brothers got to attend a number of games and loved every minute.

Thirdly, there were annual late summer skeet shoots followed by the Labor Day Dove shoot. Dad loved to shoot and believed all his sons should know gun safety and enjoy hunting as well. We all went to gun safety classes and subsequently received our own guns. Terry got a double barrel Baretta that was lighter than most guns because of his weak left arm. Two or three times in the late summer we would head out to a nearby field carrying a box of clay pigeons, a hand sling and guns for all. We all took turns slinging the clays as much like the flight of live dove as possible. Each shooter got five clays, with two shots if needed. I was very happy to get three out of five. One day our jaws flopped open when Mother said she was joining us to try her hand at the sport. She was tired of being left alone on Saturday afternoons. She watched as we all took our turns. When she said she was ready, we helped her put two or three different guns to her shoulder to see which she liked best. She picked one and we said she should try a few practice rounds to get used to the gun recoil kick, plus align her eye to the target and its speed. After a few rounds with moderate success, she announced she was ready. Shot the first two. Then the third and fourth. With much drama, we loaded her gun for the final clay. She barely nicked it, but it counted. She lay her gun down and with a big smile declared that anything this easy could not really be called a sport. She never let us live this one down.

Dove season traditionally starts the first Saturday in September before Labor Day Monday, at noon. Dad usually found the hunt which often was a few hours away and we would head out early taking two cars, all the guns, stools, bird bags, insect repellent, ear plugs, a case of ammunition, lunch, ice and drinks. We usually ate lunch with some friends we met there, then we headed out into the field together, spacing ourselves far enough apart from each other and the other hunters already in position. We set up our stools and awaited high noon and the arrival of the birds. Somebody usually shouted out the time at High Noon, and we searched the sky for the first arrival. Early in the season it is hard to be sure a bird is really a dove since you haven't seen one in a year. On Terry's first hunt, he fired his first shot and felled a bird, marched out into the field to retrieve it. Upon viewing his prize, he sadly yelled, "It's a blue jay!" Dad yelled, "Shh, the Warden will hear you!" Again, early in the season, it is hard to tell if they are flying too high out of your range, or get used to the speed, and remember to shuck your shell if you miss and take a second try. After all that, if you hit the dove, you walk out in the field, retrieve it, stuff it in your bird bag and return to your stand unless they fly over you again, then you crouch in place, stand and take your shot. The daily limit per person is 12 and if you fill out early, you can keep shooting to fill out another person's limit, like your brother's. Normally the birds don't really start flying until 4 or 4:30 p,m., and gradually build momentum until sunset when shooting must cease. This usually gives you two to two and a half hours max of good shooting. Then back to the cars, count up the birds, and start lying about the ones that got away and why you missed them in the first place. If the truth be known, Robin usually shot his limit and added another half dozen birds to others including mine. Usually we stop somewhere on the way home to eat dinner, " 'cause mama ain't cookin' no late dinner for any alleged sportsmen!" Another great Tyler Brothers' annual tradition, loved by all, even if there were no dove flying.

Continuing the sporting theme, let's turn to fishing in Canada and travel to Barney's Ball Lake Lodge way up in Ontario. Dad took us all, one by one, on a week-long fishing excursion. I was fortunate to even be invited because when I was five, Dad took me and my Zebco to a nearby pond on a blistery hot summer day with no food or water. There was one tree on the pond, but Dad didn't want me to get my line tied up in the tree. Finally, after noticing that I had turned bright beet red and was feeling faint, he relented to moving to the shade where I promptly cast my line and got it hopelessly tangled, which even wore Dad out so we could leave. Only the Coca-Cola at a nearby gas station brought me back to life. It was still a pretty quiet trip home. Only after we got into our partially air-conditioned house, did I utter my never-to-be-forgotten and always- to-be-reminded fishing trip death knell, "Dad, the next time you go fishing, I want to stay home," (a clear critical thinking blunder!). It was only later, that I learned that Mother blew Dad out for the irresponsible act of taking a five year old out in the blistering heat with no sun screen, food or water. Only by the Grace of God did Dad relent and take me to Canada. You start with a grueling two-day car trip across the border to a small town near Ontario. There you take a Sea Otter twin engine, pontoon plane, land on Ball Lake, and taxi right up to Barney's Lodge. Indians unload our bags, we walk into the Lodge where smiling Barney greets us "How was your trip, Sam?", followed by, "Who did you bring as your guide this year?"

Man, you want to talk about an absolutely beautiful part of the country and perfect set up, this was it! No wonder Dad kept coming back with one of us as his excuse. The first day, like the following two, we rise early for a great breakfast of anything we want, gather our gear, meet our Indian guides and another father and son guest team, load up our gear and head for the dock. There we load into two boats which already have coolers of drinks and food and shove off. Each metal boat is equipped with a reliable outboard, bait and fish wells. We glide across a still glassy lake with the guide driving, me next, and Dad in the front. We would see the other boat a little later when the guides wanted to exchange information about what fish were biting on what bait and where, but generally it was just us. After about a half hour, the engine slows, the bow drops, and we nestle close to the shoreline, but not too close. The guide baits our hook with a live minnow and we cast away. The guide says "Walleye," our intended prey. Dad asks if the guide wants to throw in a line; he says maybe later.

In about 20 minutes, Dad gets a nibble, sets the hook and lands about a two-pound Walleye which we all deem is too small, and back he goes. My line starts to twitch, I set the hook and reel in a three pounder deemed a keeper, and into the live fish well he dives. This is getting fun—nothing to it. By around lunchtime, we have about a dozen keepers and we head to the lake's bank for a shore lunch. We head around the corner to relieve ourselves, and return to gather firewood, but the guide has already started the fire and headed to the water to filet lunch. We open a drink and watch the procedure. The other boat appears, the guides exchange information, then out they go again. The guide shares that the other boat has caught a good catch of lake trout on the other side of the island and we would swap places for the afternoon. The guide offers up some nice looking roast beef sandwiches he has brought in case our morning luck had waned and some cookies. We passed on the sandwiches, but have just enough room left for a cookie. We douse the fire, clean up the site as if we had not landed, and speed off to our afternoon location. Within 20 minutes our lines are twitching again! Our Lake trout are not as plentiful as our walleyed pike, but bigger. By the time we are ready to head back we have bagged ten keepers which were ample. I forget the Canadian limits, but I was sure we had not broken any laws. We land back at the dock at about 5:00 pm, thank our guide, and head to the bar for an adult beverage. The Lodge is full, about 20-25 guests and we gather around the bar, swap lies and tell stories. Everybody has had a great day. We have worked up an appetite and dinner: clearly first class. Off to shower, bed and fish dreams.

 The next day was more of the same but different. Barney told us that he had a plane ready to fly us to another nearby lake that was plenty busy yesterday. He said there were bigger trout and some other varieties I wasn't familiar with. We climbed into the Otter, with the pilot and two large Indian guides with Dad in the co-pilot seat. We pulled away from the dock and began the race across the lake to take off into the wind. We gained momentum and watched the shoreline race closer and closer. Suddenly Dad reached for the throttle and jerked it back. The pilot looked over with a shy grin saying, "I was just about go do that, don't worry. Looks like we got one too many Indians." He pulled back to the dock, deposited an Indian saying not to worry that there was another flight flying our way shortly. That was my first water take-off having taken off from land when we arrived and I was a little surprised. Dad confirmed that we were in good hands with these pilots and he was not really worried. We raced across the lake again with a lightened load and ascended with ease. Within 45 minutes we were landing again and approaching the dock. We disembarked, loaded up our boat and headed out. We had lines out pretty quickly, but had chosen a spot near the center of the lake. In about another 45 minutes we saw another Otter circle, land and motor up to our boat. Dad was seriously worried that they were bringing a message from Mom about an urgent problem at home. The pilot drove up to our boat, handing a bucket to our guide with fresh bait for a full day, if things turned out to be as busy as yesterday. Dad was visibly relieved, the plane raced away, and the lines were a bobbin'. The yield was as advertised; plentiful, large, and varied, but mostly trout. Another well prepared shore lunch and another wasted sandwich. A calmer, short afternoon, but plenty of keepers. Back to camp, the bar and dinner. The next day, Barney said the choice was ours to make. Ball Lake, a repeat of yesterday, or a third site a little further away? Dad chose Ball Lake only because it meant more time fishing and less time traveling. We had plenty of traveling ahead the next two days heading home. The third day was the best of all! A fishing trip of a lifetime!

A number of years later, the Tyler brothers caucused to make our first big time group investment decision. Led by Gwathmey, it was for the four brothers and wives to host Mother and Daddy, for Dad's 60th birthday, on a fishing trip at Barney's Ball Lake lodge. Talk about gut wrenching! Four men, just starting their marriages, families and careers, dead broke, mortgaged to the gills, were just about to jump off a big cliff with no landing in sight. But it was Dad's big birthday and Mom was dying to go because she had always been left behind—and after all they had done for us. Well, the wives revolted—all on the phones to their divorce lawyers—abandonment, neglect, cruelty, bankruptcy. We had to be guilty. But your honor, we invited our wives and are therefore completely innocent. To make a long divorce cheaper, my wife Beth was the only one to attend due to the fact we had just married, had no children, and had a smallish mortgage. Everyone had a great time, no one died, divorced or declared bankruptcy. We all lived to make much bigger mistakes.

Meanwhile back at the ranch... Terry is entering sixth grade and I am in the ninth at Anchorage School in the fall of 1962. The neighborhood next door between us and the Colgans has been growing. The Macy family moved into a new house with the Colgans on one side and us on the other. Bob Macy, the oldest was in high school at Eastern and Harry, the younger son, was in ninth grade at Anchorage. Across the street in front of their house, were the Breams. Bob, the father, ran a tire store, and he was married to Mary Louise, or ML as she was called. Their oldest was ML, or Shug as we called her, my age and in ninth grade with me. She had a younger sister, Ellie, Terry's age, and Tommy, about five. Shug transferred to Sacred Heart Academy the next year and after attending U of K and became First Runner Up to Miss Kentucky. Harry Macy and Terry both liked to collect snakes, frogs, turtles and other reptiles, and they kept them in our cottage. They became pretty good friends, even though not the same age.

We were at school one Thursday morning when the Anchorage Police Car parked in the front of the school and the two policemen entered the school. After about two hours they left with a student with them. Mrs. Ewing, the principle, came on the intercom and said school would be dismissed in about an hour and that our parents had been notified to come pick us up. Mom picked up Terry and me at about 1:00 p.m. and we went straight home. We told Mother we knew the police had been at school, but we didn't know why. When we got home, Mom told us to go to our rooms and study and not go outside. She added that Dad would be coming home early and we would talk about what happened at school then. Robin came home about 4:00 pm, Dad shortly thereafter. Gwathmey was already a freshman at W&L. Dad explained that Harry Macy had been arrested by the police at school and was being held for further evaluation. He had stabbed Ellie Bream five times in the back with a five-inch pocket knife and had given Tommy a concussion by hitting him on the head with a rock in the process. He admitted he was really looking for Marie, but could not find her at the time. This had all happened late Wednesday afternoon. Dad continued that school had been suspended for Friday, so families could deal with the tragedy in their own way. He felt that Terry and I should probably stay inside, but Robin could go on to Waggener. Terry spoke up saying he and Harry were friends and he wanted to do something. Dad suggested Terry write a note to Harry proclaiming his continued friendship, and he and Mother could walk over and give it to Mrs. Macy which she should certainly appreciate. After many months of analysis and treatment, it was divulged that Harry was loved too much by his mother and he was lashing out against that unconsciously. Ellie and Tommy recovered, but Ellie suffered after effects for years. The take-away from this tragedy is that no matter how safe, rich and protected your community and family is, there is no protection from random violent acts due to undetected mental illness.

Following graduation from Anchorage School, I followed Robin to Camp Dudley, but he had decided he liked Camp Pasquaney better and went there. After a full day ride on the milk train from New York's Grand Central Station, where Anne Leduc saw me off, I arrived in Westport, New York. Not one familiar face at Camp Dudley, so I decided to strap on my helmet and make some new friends through critical thinking. They gave me my camper number (#9404), showed me to my cabin and at the completion of introductions, it was off to the dining hall with the ringing of the dinner bell. I ate a good meal at my cabin's assigned table after which we had free time which I chose to spend shooting the breeze with my new family, while arranging my things at my assigned bunk. Then brush your teeth, put on pajamas, and learn the meeting of Vespers, followed by prayers and finally bed as signaled by the Last Horn and the singing of "Now the Day is Over" in the distance. And Wow it gets cold in up state New York at night! The only thing colder is Lake Champlain for swim tryouts at the end of June. I thought I had lost my breath and "equipment" forever! I loved everything about my two seasons there, where I made some wonderful friends and memories. Beautiful country, but too far up in Yankee Land. My son loved it as well. Well worth the money.

After the Labor Day dove hunt that fall, I started at Waggener High as a sophomore, got a bid from ALA, accepted and pledged through the first of the year. Since Robin had a different schedule, Mother would pick me up every day after school. She was always inquisitive about how my day went, and whom I had met. Actually, an attractive, well-built girl had been rubbing up next to me as I exchanged the books in my locker. I told Mom that I had met a girl and was thinking of asking her out. When she inquired her name, I answered Susan Soble. This was followed by silence, then a low, "hmmm, I think you should slow that down." I responded "Meaning?" She began, "She is probably Jewish and Jews and Christians have not gotten along well for centuries. Most young Jewish girls mature faster than boys, and the Jewish girls prefer young Christian boys over their own kind. I am not saying we are anti-Jew, just saying we are not in favor of a relationship." Hmm...I just didn't think the birds and bees speech would sneak up on me like this. It turns out that my own personal experience confirmed Mom's advice. Susan and I went nowhere, but a few years later another Jewish girl did give me a little well needed and appreciated sex education. Many years later in graduate school, a good friend of ours began a serious relationship with a Jewish girl and my best friend and I were invited to be ushers in the wedding. The first night of the festivities, the groom's father came up to the both of us and offered each of us $5,000 to stop the wedding. A very enticing offer I assure you for two broke MBA graduates. We discussed a variety of plausible options, but in the end, could not convince ourselves that we would be successful. The marriage failed after eight years, thankfully before any children. Many years after that my children attended a Judeo Christian Private School and I served on the Board. After all that, I do not believe I am anti-Jew, but I do not believe that a strong Jew married to a strong Christian can last together very long, particularly after children. I am, however in a rapidly growing minority about inter-marriage of all types. Jews are rapidly becoming more secular as are Christians and inter-faith marriage is growing rapidly. The same holds true for inter-racial marriages. In 1959 only 4% of Americans approved of inter-racial marriages which remained illegal until the law changed after the Love vs Virginia ruling in 1967. By 2013, 87% of Americans approved and inter-racial marriages have increased rapidly. As we know over this same period divorces have been steadily on the rise. I have no data on inter-racial vs. inter-faith divorce rates or causes. From personal experience, however, I know that spouses holding opposing strong political beliefs cannot co-exist for long. Although strong political beliefs are seemingly on the rise in the U.S., I believe intensity of political beliefs, like religious beliefs, are moving rapidly toward secularism and the great American melting pot has finally arrived. This is a long journey through my critical thinking that is hopefully as deep as it will get!

SOPHOMORE YEAR AT WAGGENER

While I was in Germany, I turned 16 and was legal to drive upon my return. One Saturday in September, Dad knocked on the door of a tidy house in a tidy neighborhood he passed by every day to and from work. For over a year he had been eyeing a 1955 blue and white Chevrolet Biscayne parked on the street. Never garaged as far as Dad knew, it was none the worse for wear. A man answered the door and when asked, responded that he had not planned on selling it but would take a reasonable cash offer. Dad said he was prepared to write the man a check for x amount if he would let Dad take it to his mechanic, check it out and return it by 3 p.m. The man looked at the check, agreed to the price and handed Dad the key. Now Dad had owned a few cars and had a great relationship with a mechanic, who took the car, promising a reliable response in two hours. Dad went to lunch, returning at 2 p.m. The mechanic volunteered that the car was indeed in excellent shape and that Dad had offered a bargain price. Dad paid the mechanic and returned in the car to the house. The owner shyly admitted that he had talked to his wife and he had decided that for the trouble of not having a car for a while, the price was about x+10%. Dad responded that the price increase was fine and he would return with a new check in an hour with another driver to drive the car home. Dad arrived home looking for Robin, who was not there, and drove off with Mom to finalize the purchase. When Robin and I drove up the drive after spending the day at an ALA work party, we spotted the beauty and ran into the house. Mom and Dad were having a pre-dinner drink when we came busting in. Dad calmly stood up, handed me the key, gave me a hug and wished me a Happy Birthday and Merry Christmas. As he turned to mix another drink, I thanked him and Robin and I ran back outside to give her a quick inspection and spin around the block.

Now, it needs to be said that Dad was ahead of his time when it came to child rearing. He used "Trust, but Verify" long before Ronald Reagan, whom he later voted for. Teach his sons how to drive and keep doing it. Teach his sons how to drink responsibly and keep doing it. Admittedly it took a lot of patience and trust on his part.

I was proud of that car, washed her every week, vacuumed her every other, and waxed her quarterly. One Saturday night, we double dated to the drive-in. It was so hot in the car, one couple sat on the bumper and one on the roof, legs draped onto the windshield, and traded off. It was a fun night. I was waking up the next morning and Dad came in like most mornings and raised the window shades making sure each was exactly even with the other while he got dressed for work. "Where in Hell did you go last night?" he asked in a very grumpy tone. "We went to the drive-in" I blurted, bounding from the bed to the window, beside Grumpy. I looked down at my car and spotted two, soup bowl like impressions on my roof. I mumbled, "You can't see 'em from the ground." Grumpy stomped out of the room and mumbled back, "Stupid, don't ever try that again!" Back in the dog house!

When fall came, I was busy with ALA work parties and had followed Robin as a Waggener High varsity football manager. Practice every day after school, games every Friday night. We had a very good squad and won every game. It was the end of November and we were headed for the State Championship on Friday night with a pep rally set for 3 p.m. At 2:30 p.m., Principal Duncan came on the intercom, "CBS News has just informed us that (I thought he was going to say the Championship would be carried live on Channel five), President John F. Kennedy had been shot to death in Dallas, Texas. Please bow your head for a silent prayer." The air left the room. What could be next? "Please assemble in the gymnasium for more announcements." Everyone was in shock. A million questions raced through my head. We all headed in silence for the gym. The decorations, signs and streamers for the rally looked eerily silly, girls were crying and hugging one another. We all found a seat. Principal Duncan said a prayer for the nation and we all stood for the National Anthem. At the conclusion, Principal Duncan informed us that the Championship had been postponed for a week and that the meeting was adjourned. I made my way to Sherry, a cheerleader I had a date with that night, took her home, and said I would pick her up at seven to get a bite to eat unless her parents had some objection. I went home, talked to my parents, called my ALA friend I was doubling with that night, showered and left. I picked up my friend and his date first, then Sherry, and headed for the Frisch's Big Boy. I don't like being sad and everyone around me being sad. Sometimes, funny guy, I felt like it was my job to lighten everybody up. We pulled into the order-and-eat-in- your-car spot, and I, in my tested and trusted best JFK accent, spoke into the microphone "Iye would like, uh, two bougers, two fryies and, uh, two cokes and uh, Byobby what are, uh , you and Ethel having?" Not a laugh or even a smile anywhere, especially from Sherry! I fell flat on my face. Things were even more somber than before. Poor critical thinking and in bad taste. We ate our meal in relative silence and called it an early night.

At the first of the year, Robin became the first Tyler ever to be elected President of ALA. We were all proud of him, and I spent the winter and spring working hard at ALA work parties, cutting and delivering firewood. Early summer was not to be the most pleasant. Dr. Fischer, my orthopedist, announced that since I was now grown, I needed to have my, polio leg operated on so I could walk better the rest of my adult life. He sent me to a foot and hand specialist, Dr. Kleinert, who was building quite the reputation. He was noted for very complex procedures, many requiring several surgeons, lasting late into the night, where he would go to sleep on the operating table and begin at 8 a.m. the next morning. It turned out that my foot would be one of last he would do, before he began specializing only in hands and becoming world renowned. My operation required lengthening my heel chord, freezing my ankle in place so it could not wobble from side to side, straightening all my toes so they would not curl up, assisted by running steel pins through the joints and left ones hanging out of the front. Then a plaster cast was wrapped around the leg to let it set in place, crafted so the toes were left in the open, protected by a bumper. As you might imagine, working with all these bones, was quite painful and I remember as I was coming out of the anesthetic Dad whispering in my ear to try to bear the pain so I could get off the heroin I was taking. It was very painful, and I stayed in the hospital four days to work through it and the nausea from the extended length of the operation. It had lasted over six hours and had been judged a success. I was fitted for crutches and released. I was up walking with the crutches at home in three days. The relative cool of June became the sweltering heat of July. The not-so-funny kid at the pool ran off with my crutches as I sunned, and the guard retrieved them. A knitting needle wedged between the leg and cast relieved the itch of healing. The Doc swapped the old cast for a "walker" after a satisfactory x-ray permitted it. Relief came to my forearms and underarms, as I eased off the crutches. He said I could swap everything for a leg brace the first of August. Good Old ALA. Three frat brothers Jimmy Forrester, his older brother Chase who had been in an iron lung from polio at the same time Terry and I were dealing with it, Harry Fuller and Chase's black companion, caregiver and wing man, Mike, had rented a cottage for three weeks in Charlevoix, Michigan, in August and I was invited as an extra driver. Harry was recovering from a summer knee operation from a football injury and would ride with me, designated chaperone; Mike, would drive the Forrester brothers. My cast came off, my brace was forged and fitted, and we headed North. Upon arrival we stocked the fridge with beer and loaded up on party food. We had the ideal batch-pad-on the lake, in the middle of the action, and a perfect party-till-you-drop layout. We made a few calls locating the party for the first night and headed out right after a quick dinner. Plenty of bodacious babes were there for the duration. Things were clearly looking up! To fully appreciate this outing, you really need to know Chase. He was an experienced cripple on the make. He had taken karate with the only working muscle in his upper torso, his neck. While sitting in his chair he would call you close, whispering in your ear and would sling you across the room with a splitting headache, all in a split second with black belt precision. Intimidating. You could be at a deb party and think it was raining as you looked across the room and spotted Chase, seated in his chair, with a drink on his tray and straw in his mouth. The perfect aim of a Navy Seal sniper. That man never wanted for respect, admiration or genuine love from his troops.

    Lucky me, I snagged my date for the duration on the first night. Maggie Kuhn was very attractive, with a great sense of humor, from Indianapolis, Indiana, and lived right next to us. She fixed everyone else up with her friends.

She had spent plenty of summers here, knew all the places to go and what to do, and when. Now back to Chase. He taught us that all women are generous and curious, particularly about a good-looking man, paralyzed from the neck down. Is he really paralyzed down there too? Only one way to find out! And they all did. They all came out smiling. And my date smiled too and kept them coming. It was a great and memorable three weeks. My first, semi-chaperoned, sleep over adventure with more to come. I think I am going to like this. After returning home, Maggie and I enjoyed several home and away weekends together but sadly realized that summer romances cannot survive long over long distances.

Robin graduated from Waggener in the Spring, and attended Guilford College, or Quaker Tech, as he called it, in Greensboro, North Carolina. But not before another hilarious event along the way. Probably the finest, fanciest new car Dad ever owned was a midnight blue, two door Buick Riviera coupe with midnight blue interior, buckets up front and center console automatic shift. Robin and Dad took it on Robin's college tour, ending up in Winston Salem staying with an old college buddy of Dad's, Jimmy Foltz. He had a fine-looking daughter exactly Robin's age, that he deemed worthy of a ride in the Riviera for a drink after dinner, while the 'rents sipped a few more scotches and reminisced about the Duke Blue Devils. Now Robin has been known to become amorous after a few, which can be contagious. One thing led to another, he behind the wheel, she in his lap, perched precariously on the center console. Robin is rounding second, heading to third when suddenly the mood is broken by a scream as she leaps up swatting her rear end. Turns out she had perched on the cigarette lighter, depressing it until it became red hot, burning through her dress and tattooing her back side. They were laughing themselves to tears, but mood broken, decided to return home. They had hoped to sneak into their assigned bedrooms unnoticed, but no such luck. Caught by the now drunken Blue Devils, they were shamed into divulging their dastardly deeds and all nearly ended up on the floor laughing. Another one for the comic books.

One more, big brother blooper. Gwathmey returned home for summer break from W&L and we all sat down together again for a formal candle lit, "Viola served," Saturday night dinner. Our distinguished guest utters "Pass the F---ing butter, please": Robin coughs, I spew out my milk laughing, and Dad growls, "Nice frat gutter talk, Gwathmey. Is that what they teach now at the SAE house at W&L? What have you got to say for yourself?" "I'm sorry, please pass the butter" he muttered. Lesson learned; note to self—best zip your lip when you return home from college!

Sometime right around here, Dad decided to sell Nanny's house in town and invest it into a suite off of the den. She became a regular and it gave Mom and Dad a chance to travel to see friends and clients. She was becoming "hard of hearing" and would sit up close to the speaker on the side of the TV rather than in front of the screen. One night at dinner, Nanny was at the head, Robin to her right with me to her left, the parents out of town. "Now boys, I'm hearing better today and I want you to speak at a normal level to see if I am right," she boasted. Somehow Robin knew to the decibel what she could and could not hear. He looks at me and mumbles, "Billy, did you pick up the condoms at the drug store today, like I asked you?" I about spewed a mouthful! "Now, now, I said speak normally don't mumble," she admonished...thankfully. Several years later, Robin brought his to-be bride, Marty, home for the big announcement. They found themselves alone with Nanny in the living room. "Marty, 'wanna go up in my bedroom and get a little?" Marty dove under the couch. Nanny didn't move. Robin still had his touch!

The fall of 1964, my senior year in high school. Robin and Gwathmey were gone--just Terry and I. We drew closer, working ALA work parties together and even double dating some. I was elected President of ALA, most likely because I was President Robin's, and Gwathmey's little brother. In October, a tragic accident I will never forget occurred. It was late Saturday afternoon; I was driving Mother's station wagon because ALA brother Sam Harvey and I were delivering

firewood together. Sam was a starting forward on the Waggener varsity basketball team, already a top college prospect.

We were driving past Bauer's Bar, one of Dad's favorite haunts, on the way to take Sam home before that night's ALA meeting. Suddenly a car turned left in front of me with no warning. We collide, Sam launches through the windshield, then collapses, back into my lap. Blood everywhere, I somehow reach into my pocket, pull out a handkerchief and wipe the blood from Sam's face. His nose slides across his face. I carefully slide it back. My door opens, someone asks if I can move. I nod my head and struggle from behind the wheel, trying not to disturb Sam's head. I suggest that we wait for the medics before moving Sam, if the traffic has been stopped. Sirens wail, I sit on another car's fender and determine that all the blood on me must be Sam's. The medics carefully load Sam onto a stretcher and into an ambulance. The medic inquires as to my condition; I indicate fine, other than a couple of bruises. He suggests that I am probably in shock, to remain seated and drink the water he hands me. Another ALA buddy arrives and asks if he can take me home. I climb into his car after I take a hard look at Mom's totaled wreck as it is being loaded onto the wrecker. I arrive home to face the music. After explaining the full circumstances, and convincing them I was fine, Dad offered that Robin had just called to divulge that he had totaled his car but was fine. Dad looked at Mom and says, "Claudia, if we get a call from London, you take it!" The next day, I visited Sam in the hospital. He was fully bandaged, was not sure what had happened, and was depressed as he contemplated sitting on the bench for the rest of the season. During his operation, they confirmed Sam's nose was attached by a thread, sutured all the way around the rest of his nose, and took his contact lenses out of his eyes. Sam recovered in time to play a handful of games at the end of the season, and secured a full basketball scholarship to the University of Virginia. All's well that ends well, I guess.

Back at school, I was elected, VP of the senior class, enjoyed being Sports Editor of "The Chit-Chat," Waggener's school newspaper. I even snagged an interview with the legendary coach of the winning University of Kentucky basketball Wildcats, Adolph Rupp. In the fall, I was still managing the football team which had a decent record. One particularly cold Friday night, my friend Chase from last summer was wheeled onto the field by his companion, Mike, and we enjoyed the game together. At the end, we waited for the crowd to thin, and I drove my car onto the field to pick everyone up. Sherry, the cheerleader, was my date that night and she climbed in front with me, Chase was next to her with Mike in the back seat after he had placed Chase's chair in the trunk. I climbed behind the wheel, rubbing my hands together, trying heat 'em up. Sherry reached over and took my hands depositing them between her warm thighs, whispering "I can help with that." I responded with, "Oohwee that is much better, Chase you need your hands warmed?" He followed with a quick "yeah!" Sherry took his paralyzed cold hands and placed them next to mine. We drove off the field, unloaded Chase, his chair, and Mike at their car. We followed them to our ALA party for that night. I kissed Sherry, and mentally promised to reward her that night for generously helping my paralyzed friend.

Memberships in the German Club and Beta Club rounded out my college applications. My grades were stellar, but my SAT scores were borderline, as I painfully learned the next year at W&L. I also was accepted to Vanderbilt but decided against it because it seemed half of my class was going there already. To me, the most gratifying accomplishment my senior year was earning election as President of ALA for the second term. This had never been done in recent memory and at the end of the year, the club awarded me the Metal Man Shield that had never been seen by any member in our family. Yes, the rest of the family had laid a foundation, but I felt this was a validation of who I had become. Success and trust among your peers is unparalleled, but also fleeting.

That summer it was back to the Chalfonte, where I was becoming and old-timer. But this year I brought along my ALA buddies Tom Tyrrell, Harry Fuller and Leland Hulbert to fill some night watchmen and bellman slots. We raised so much hell, I hoped we would be invited back!

This year is both the end of one era, and the beginning of another, deserving some reflection. The Billy years are over and I have matured to the Bill years! Robin lives in Greensboro, Gwathmey is in London, and in just two short years, Dad, Mom, Nanny, Terry and I (nominally) will live in Saint Louis, Missouri. The Anchor is out of Anchorage! For the very first time it occurs to me that I may not actually spend the rest of my life in bucolic Anchorage, Kentucky! The Tyler brothers are splitting up! In just a few months Gwathmey will be getting married and just a few years after that the Tyler brothers will enter a 50-plus year era of phenomenal growth maintaining an .84% annual rate, surpassing Louisville's rate of .75% and U.S.'s rate of .60%. And the Tyler Dynasty will be an amazing 80% male! Hold on. The fun is just beginning!

W&L AWAKENING

First, let's get to W&L. I load up the old Chevy with Dad's Navy trunk filled with my life's belongings. The rest of the old girl is filled with scavenged, junk furniture I hoped would prove useful. Then I head down the driveway and head east on highway 60 trying to sniff back the tears. Then after about eight hours without an inch of Interstate highway yet, I arrive in Lexington, Virginia and head for my assigned freshman dorm. I begin unpacking and meet my new next-door neighbor and soon to become best friend, Jim Philpott. The next day we head down the road for a three-day orientation they call Freshman Camp at Natural Bridge, where we learn all about upcoming fraternity rush, registration, class schedules, traditions, rules, etc. And before I forget it, freshmen are not allowed to have cars at school, so I parked the Chevy at Stuart and French Anderson's house. He was a distant relative of Dad's who taught electrical engineering (whatever that is) at neighboring VMI. Gwathmey had paid them a couple of visits in his four years to placate Dad. I maybe, paid them four and made sure I reported their health back to Dad each time. New brainchild Bill decided he wanted to be a doctor, so I sign up for the pre-med curriculum, the second hardest in the school. Thank goodness the first semester classes are all required for graduation from all majors anyway. Now back at the dorm, we head to the bookstore to buy the 100 lbs. of required textbooks which are one of many protected monopolies I will meet in my lifetime, requiring more money than you can ever imagine (call home immediately)!

Rush week begins and classes start later. I got invited to several fraternity parties, but quickly narrowed it to Phi Delta Theta, SAE and Beta. All three asked me to join, but the SAEs kept asking me about my older brother who was not initiated until after graduation. I got tired of this, so I chose Beta because they seemed most interested in me. Every night was heavy drinking. Sunday night, I took one sip of alcohol and immediately vomited. The next day at the infirmary I was diagnosed with hypersensitivity to alcohol, not unheard of after rush week. When asked about the expected duration, the response was a day, week, month, year, or the rest of my life. I could drink after a week, but have been cautious ever since. Now having been in a fraternity before, I was privy to all the secret handshakes, and mystic mysteries that they tried to put over on us. It was all pretty anticlimactic. As a pledge class unity project, we stole into the frat house at about 3 a.m. one Saturday night and locked everyone in his bed room after first throwing in all sorts of lit firecrackers. As we hightailed our exit up the hill, we looked back and saw curtains in several rooms were on fire. Our fastest runners returned to aid the escape of many, but were caught in the process. To show our solidarity we all returned to a rather angry beating. We were looking forward by then to a return to classes.

The Awakening appeared rather quickly and with painful consistency. Midterms arrived—one F, two D's, a C, and a B in English. Finals were almost no better with one D rising to a C-minus. I was failing out of school! One semester more of this and I would be history. And to be honest I was busting my ass, and in the library every night studying. Dean Frank Gilliam was Dean of Admissions, a dollar a year man, having married a beautiful DuPont. He was loved and revered by everyone who ever set foot on the campus and I had met him several times during the admission process. I was about to get to know him better. I was summoned to appear in his office the next day. I put on my best shirt, tie, and jacket and was headed to my day of reckoning when my good friend Jim Philpott stopped me, asking if I might look even better if my shoes matched?! In Louisville, everyone wore dress/casual lace up shoes in black or brown made by Bass and they were dubbed "Louisville Walkers" at W&L. I could barely tie them as I switched them. I walked into the Dean's office, he stood, shook my hand, and motioned me to be seated facing him at his large mahogany desk. "Now Bill," he started with a friendly smile, "I know you, your parents, brother Gwathmey, first cousin Bob Colgan, and am surprised to see you here." My head is hanging pretty low by now. "Now let's just take a look at your SAT scores." He turned around and retrieved a large bound book from his credenza behind him. He leafed through it until he found my entry and stared at it and looked up smiling, "You know what, you are doing pretty damn good! Now get out of here and turn those grades around and if I can do anything to help you just call." We stood, shook hands, I said as firmly as I could, "Yes, Sir and thank you," getting out while the getting was good! Despite the dressing down, I still merited an invitation for dinner with Dean Gilliam and his wife at their beautiful home just off campus later that semester. The next semester, my grades improved slightly, but I was on probation having failed calculus. I repeated the course at U of L over the summer, was given a C but still did not understand it. The next year, I lived in the Beta House located just down the hill from the Colonnade and library. I switched majors to Sociology, because it sounded easy and had the most electives which I carefully chose looking for the easiest. Mostly I chose English, journalism, more sociology, and since I had spent one summer in Germany, German. I lived in the library. Somehow, I was going to get through that school or die trying. I barely saw my fraternity brothers and almost never dated. Some lights began to come on. I realized that 70% of my class had gone to private school, and only 30% had gone to public. The 70% had taken all these courses the year before! They only attended courses half the time the first year, partied all weekend and started cutting class the second year. Before too long their grades began to look like mine. I had had the Freshman Crash and they were entering the Sophomore Slump. I couldn't afford to look up. The start of the winter semester was always what was called Fancy Dress Weekend sponsored by the University and doubled by the fraternities. W&L was all male at the time; most of the dates were from surrounding girls' schools, but many came from farther away for this special party weekend and all stayed overnight, three nights at local private housing for girls only. Unfortunately, this year we were treated to three feet of heavy snowfall, making the mountain roads impassable and airports unusable. The girls, who made it in by Thursday were ok. Those from farther away and arriving by air, like my date, were not. Might as well just study. Saturday noon, I trudged up the hill through three feet of snow to see the posting of the math grades of all those who passed the exam. My name was not on the list, even though I read it four times. Later my professor told me, "I have never seen anyone study this course any more than you have. You just don't get it, do you?" I trudged back down the hill. The parties started, the liquor flowed, the bands started playing. I sat studying in my room at the Beta House, never being more depressed or lonely than then, before or since. A famous remark by comedian George Gobel seems uniquely apropos here, "Sometime the whole world seems to be a tuxedo, and you are just a pair of brown shoes." The tick, tick, tick of critical thinking fades in the silence. Tinker Bell is dying. It didn't help that Lyndon B. Johnson whipped Barry Goldwater in the 1964 election. An event that year of little note, oft forgotten was the Goldwater Rule. It states that psychiatrists should not comment on the mental health of individuals whom they have not personally examined. An article was published in 1964 that more than 1,000 psychiatrists believed Sen. Barry Goldwater to be mentally unfit for the job of president. All this eventually led to the 25th amendment dealing with what to do with an incapacitated President (in play today with President Trump). The natives were restless in Alabama and the war drums were beating in Vietnam. The whole world was crashing around me. I learned later that you have to have failure before you can achieve lasting success. I can assure you, the farthest thought from my mind then was success.

Perhaps the most worn out expression is that it is always darkest just before the dawn. Well, this damn dawn sure was slow in coming. It was mid semester after the thaw, when the first glimmer of hope appeared. My math professor showed he had a kind soul, when he showed that I had not failed the class by failing the exam. I had to keep my nose to the stone and make it through the semester with a passing grade. You would think that by taking this course twice by now I could at least learn that much. I stopped by the professor's office to let him know I was grateful, continuing to work hard, and was on the same page as he as to what the end of the semester needed to look like.

I then decided to commence therapy for my brain. While in the library studying I would go to the music lab, put on the head phone and listen to the broadest selection I could find. I started with classical—Bach, Beethoven, Tchaikovsky Mozart, Chopin, Schubert, Strauss, Verdi, The Nutcracker, etc. I was amazed at how many melodies I recognized. Then more modern, George Gershwin, American in Paris, Dave Brubeck; then New Orleans Jazz; The Preservation Hall Jazz Band, Pete Fountain, Louis Armstrong, and finally the Big

Band Sound—Benny Goodman, Artie Shaw, Tommy Dorsey. I would play them over and over again. Loading fodder for critical thinking, I guess. Of course, I did not shirk studies in my required courses. The semester came to an end and my grades were a D, two C's and two B's. One important footnote to that "B": it was in English and it was made possible by a paper about my polio episode and it was awarded a rare "A". My debut of critical thinking may have been the only thing that prevented me from flunking out of school. I was still on probation, but I had not flunked out. No summer school required and back to my friend the Chalfonte for another summer, maybe my last.

W&L JUNIOR YEAR

W&L *junior year*. Gil Burke, Upton Richards—Beta brothers—and I rent an off-campus house, controlled the previous year by Louisville friend Renny Logan. We still take our meals at the Beta House. I started to date again—Hollins one hour to the south; Mary Baldwin, an hour to the north; and Sweetbriar to the east—all excellent women's colleges. And then there was Southern Seminary for Girls, 15 minutes away in Buena Vista—a finishing school at best. The first three months of school, the girls were not allowed to date or leave the campus. That next weekend the W&L cars were lined up around the block. It was like shooting fish in a rain barrel.

It was a sunny fall, big party weekend starting at noon with a keg party in Red Square, surrounded on three sides by the Beta, Phi Delta Theta, and Pi Kappa Alpha, houses. I had a date lined up from one of the girls' schools, being retrieved by a fraternity brother who returned with four. The House Boy (Chief of Staff), a jovial black called JM, short for John Marshall (probably related to "The John Marshall") and I were on the front porch of the Beta House where I had just returned from the ABC store having purchased my weekend supplies. He said, "Money (he gave us all funny nick names he thought fit us—he knew, I was going to make a lot of money), the saddest thing I have ever seen at this House, was on a day just like this, when your cousin Bob Colgan came running up these concrete steps, tripped, and broke both bottles of Jim Beam he had bought for the weekend. He just sat there on the top step, with his chin cupped in his hands, watching his entire weekend flow down the steps. Bobby finished his college studies at The University of Louisville and married Mary Clarke, who Mom immediately fell in love with and they remained fast friends. They moved to Dallas where Bobby got a job with Champion Paper Company. Over four short years, Bobby was a VP and a family of three boys, Bobby, Sammy and Chris. Suddenly, however, all five showed up with a horse van at Mom and Dad's last year when they lived in St. Louis. Bob wanted to raise those boys like he was raised, in the sunshine and on horses. They were headed to Colorado, where Bobby bought a dude ranch to breed, break and train quarter and cutting horses as well as border collies. They all lived happily ever after. When Bobby's ashes were placed in their crypt, Mary led us in singing "Happy Trails to You" which was fitting and memorable.

My date arrived, was delightful, attractive and ready to party. The keg party morphed into dinner at the Beta House, which was followed by a combo party sponsored jointly with our neighbors, the Phi Delts. The "combo" that played was a live black band, named "the Little Boys" who rapidly became regulars on Fraternity Row. They comprised a lead guitar player, bass guitar, wild drummer, two trumpets, a trombone, and both a male and female singer. They could play any song you had ever heard, better than the hit recording artist. They were the best band I had ever seen or heard! The next morning it was Bloody Marys and Beta Brunch at the House. Mid- afternoon, I took three of four girls back to their campus and returned. A great weekend, I was back!

Late one Saturday morning, I was sitting in the Beta living room awaiting lunch when the pay phone in the phone closet rang. A pledge answered it, yelled "Tyler." I rose, took the receiver, pulling the door to so I could hear. Mother, "Billy, what were you doing driving motorcycles in high school when you knew it was forbidden!!" She was right—no motorcycles, no private planes—not covered by insurance. I asked her if she knew what a Honda 90 was? She of course said no. I continued describing it as about the size of a regular bicycle, with a small motor that would make it go about the same speed as a fast bike. A friend of Robin's and mine owned a piece of the rental shop in the park and needed to have some miles put on a few new bikes, so we were just helping a friend, as we were always taught. She responded that I was wrong and should not have done it, and she was going to discuss it with Dad. I said I was sorry and inquired if there was anything else on her mind. She declined, we said our "I love you's" and hung up. Terry, had obviously been caught doing something wrong and came back with the old argument that parents always think their other sons were angels when they were not! Put it on the "get even list" with Terry.

Both 1968 and 1969 were critical years in U.S. politics: the war in Vietnam and in race relations. As for W&L, let's set the scene. It was the era of the seven o'clock news either with Chet Huntley and David Brinkley on NBC, or Walter Cronkite on CBS. Every night, most of the Beta House was sitting on dilapidated couches, digesting dinner in the darkened TV room in the basement, tuned to Walter Cronkite. The major event during my time was the Vietnam War, started in 1955 but escalated heavily in 1963. College students lived in fear of their draft number being called or failing out of school and immediately being drafted no matter what their number was. Every night we watched the carnage. Every month we each knew at least one more friend called to war. In April 1968, Martin Luther King was assassinated in Memphis. Immediately race riots broke out in 110 U.S. cities, led by Washington, Baltimore and Chicago. In May, W&L held their famous Mock Election vote for the candidate they felt would be nominated as the presidential candidate from the then party out of power. Richard M. Nixon won the W&L vote, which had been proven correct 75% of the time in previous years. Robert F. Kennedy was assassinated June 5, 1968 in Los Angeles, California. On July 16, Richard M. Nixon overcame George Romney, Nelson Rockefeller, Ronald Reagan and Charles Perry for the Republican nomination at the Cow Palace in Daley City, California, won nine of thirteen state primaries and chose Spiro Agnew as his running mate. In early August, President LBJ called a halt to the bombing in the Vietnam War. On August 27, Hubert Humphrey won the Democratic nomination in Atlantic City, Maryland, choosing Senator Edmund Muskie as his running mate. On November 5, Richard M. Nixon won the election, taking 32 states, 301 electoral votes but a close popular margin of 31,800,000 to 31,272,000. George Wallace won five Southern states. To summarize, seven history making events including two assassinations, riots in 110 cities, three presidential candidates and three separate elections separated by less than 500,000 votes in an eight-month period. It is hard to believe that any period in history was more contentious than today, but 1968 America was, and thank goodness there were only two major news networks instead of today's twenty. The 1968 W&L Mock Convention held in the gymnasium consisted of speeches from national political leaders on Thursday night, a parade through town Friday afternoon featuring bands, state floats, honorary kings and queens, confetti, trinkets—the whole megillah. Full blown nominating speeches and state roll call votes from state delegations with their state placards and standards took place on schedule and a winner was chosen Saturday morning, all punctuated by fraternity combo parties into the night. All of this was preceded by almost a year of meetings with every state delegation in each state by the W&L appointed state delegate to try to determine who that state would be voting for in the actual convention. This was not a popularity contest but an exhaustive effort to get it right. I did not lead the Kentucky delegation, but solicited significant cash contributions to the overall mock convention and gave it my all on mock convention week. You could not do this if you didn't love politics as I did ever since meeting Nixon in person. It also helped if your date for the weekend could tolerate your enthusiasm, which thankfully mine did. Clearly the mock convention was the high point of my junior year—matched only by making the good Dean's list at semester's close.

Before plowing into senior year, let's stop and get to know my housemates a little better. Upton Hill Richards was a graduate of Fauquier County High School in Warrenton, Virginia where he played guard on the high school basketball team. He lived across the hall from me in the freshman dorm. He tried out for the W&L Generals but sprained his ankle and never made the team which pretty well depressed him all of our freshman year. He got a bid to Beta which he accepted and we pledged together. James Gilliam Burke resided in Mount Airy, Surry County, North Carolina, and graduated from Mt. Airy High School. He never ever played a team sport, but hunted the hounds regularly on fox hunts on his mighty Jumper, Mandit. Mandit joined Gilly, as we called him, his sophomore year and was stabled in Rockbridge where they rode regularly. He drove the sexiest car in the class—a shiny new, steel gray, GTO with black bucket seats that he drove like a bat out of hell. He looked like a rider—about six feet, strong thighs, big, high butt. He had a million sayings—my favorite, "Well, butter my butt and call me a biscuit." But Gil's most amazing strength and asset was his innate intelligence. He never studied. He was a pre-med major and the night before the ball-buster organic chemistry exam that culls the ranks at all pre-med programs, he played cards all night in the Beta card room.

Poker was never played in the card room, only Boo-Ray, a New Orleans game which required remembering which cards had been played and which had not—something Gil was a wizard at. Housemate Upton was nearly the opposite of Gil. Shy, introvert, average smarts, non-athletic, history major. The way Gil and I summed it up was we needed somebody to listen and laugh at our jokes. In many ways, our house was a microcosm of the full Beta House—a random collection of totally different personalities and talents. The President of the student body was a Beta. The Beta House was on social probation nearly all the time. The faculty and administration were stumped. Let's take a look at just a few characters, mostly from my class. Two guys from Chattanooga Coca-Cola bottling money who married each other's sisters and ended up on the Board, only because they were loaded. The pervert from Pensacola who would intimidate everyone by pulling out his Johnson at inopportune times—usually in front of our dates. To our amazement he dated the same beautiful girl all four years, but she ended up marrying another fraternity brother. Our pervert was almost disbarred from the Florida Bar years later for the same practice. There was one very bright brother from Houston and another pre-med major from Jasper, Alabama. One guy from up east was expelled his freshman year for having a girl in his dorm room after hours, and was readmitted our senior year after that rule had been rescinded. Finally, an underclassman from South Carolina, who was given a bid after rush week, so he could be ridiculed by the Chattanooga duo and Pensacola pervert. He seemed to relish the attention which made it worse and extended his immaturity and inferiority complex. He would give a show at parties biting off the top of beer bottles. When the Dean of Students asked him if the rumors of him eating glass were true, he responded with "No sir, just chew it." They even printed hundreds of bumper stickers with "Pray for (blank's) Baby." Just about all the girl's schools passed around the advice to avoid the Beta House at all costs. Only the bold, brave and beautiful walked through our doors!

A few words about my favorite classes and major. I was a Sociology major and Journalism minor. There are three separate Schools at W&L, the school of Commerce (or "C" School); the School of Journalism; and the graduate School of Law. The harder undergraduate school and most respected is the "C" School. Take note—I did not major or minor in the harder school! Dr. James Leyburn, a true Renaissance man, was the Head of the Sociology Department. He was a classical pianist, giving at least one concert a year, most years. He took notes in Latin while reading Greek and vice versa. His Introduction to Sociology lectures were in a stadium seating style room, and attracted over 90 students with a waiting list. He required two papers a year, which were usually handed in after his Wednesday lecture and returned on Friday. Mine was twenty pages typed, double spaced. He corrected all spelling and punctuation and had comments on each page regarding content, adding some specific guidance on improvement. My overall grade was A-. The man was a true genius. At varying times, he was Dean of Students, Dean of the School, Provost and Assistant to the President. My guess is he was gay and liberal, but I didn't notice things like that back then. Next to this series, I liked the lectures on propaganda offered in the School of Journalism. They covered the movements for Independence, different countries around the world; Nazism; Communism; Socialism all the way up to the modern era in newspapers, magazines, radio and television. In retrospect, I wish I had taken more U.S. History, some philosophy, political science and "C "School courses. Neither math nor memorization was my strength.

Now feeling comfortable about courses, grades and housemates, I wanted to move toward more steady dating and an eye toward the future and post-graduation. Gil and I were really best friends and he suggested dating a girl named Engle Yokely from his hometown of Mt. Airy and now a senior at Mary Baldwin College. Since she had grown up with Gil, maybe she wouldn't think The Betas was the animal house it was. We started dating at the beginning of the Semester. What made it more fun was that my oldest friend from Louisville, Peter Kintz, who pledged me at ALA and at the Beta house was now in the Law School, and had started dating a suite-mate of Engle's. Pete lived just up the hill from the Beta House in the church rectory with another Beta Law student Pete (Pete and Re-Pete) Hendricks. Kintz and I carpooled every weekend, the girls both stayed in their mandated and approved housing. We all became one happy little family. Engle had striking features, was a good dresser and dancer. She had simple tastes. What was not to like? Her father owned a furniture company, her mother was attractive, and they lived in a well- appointed home. Before too long, Gil, Engle and I drove to Mt. Airy for the weekend and I met the whole crowd. Things got more and more comfortable. I started thinking about maybe something more permanent after graduation.

It was time for my graduation. I had secured a job paying a fair wage at a bank in Louisville, and I was proud that unlike Gwathmey, I did not have to call the parents with my final grades and give them the green light to attend. The whole family showed up and fell in love with Engle. After all the festivities were over and everyone had gone home, I drove down to Mt. Airy to pop the BIG Question. It did not go well. No hard feelings, but she wasn't ready to settle down.

We parted friends and I headed back to Lexington. Now rethinking post-graduation, I decided I really wanted to get an MBA. Dad had a goal of sending us all on a trip to Europe after graduation, which he had done for Gwathmey. I asked him if I could apply those funds to an MBA if I raised the rest of the money through scholarships or debt and he agreed. I took the required, post-graduate exam and applied to all the normal schools in the Southeast to which W&L graduates historically applied to and was turned down by them all. Their reasoning was sound and consistent. They believed you could contribute more in classes and thus get more out of them if you first had work experience, which usually meant at least two years. OK, now I needed a paying job for a year or two. Plan B. Somehow, Farris Hotchkiss, the Director of Development and I had started up a dialogue—likely initiated by my old friend and fan, Dean Gilliam. Farris explained that they were looking for an assistant director and head of the annual giving fund. The Board of Directors were ready to begin a major capital drive and wanted to see a team. I told Farris I would like to get a starting salary close to what the Louisville Bank had offered. He agreed with only one catch. The President of the University, Bob Huntley, and he wanted someone who could make a five-year commitment. I told him five years was a long, long time and that I really wanted to get an MBA. I said you may not like me and I may not like you or this kind of work. I knew I was up to the task and demands of the job, but I could not, in good faith, make a five year commitment and I didn't think anyone else could either. I ended with the thought that we be honest with each other and see how we both felt after a year. He said he was OK with that and he would try to sell it to Bob Huntley. The next day he said Bob had reluctantly agreed and we had a deal. I still think Dean Frank Gillum was somehow involved.

Plan B was looking good. I moved out of my house into my apartment on the banks of the scenic Maury River. Even the curtains worked. Bought a few things besides beer for the fridge. Learned how to cook. Yuck, I hated maturity already. The next week, I moved into my not so spacious personal office in historic Washington Hall in the middle of the Colonnade with President Huntley just around the corner and up the stairs. I had a mahogany desk, a window and private phone (desktop computers had not yet been invented). Just outside my door were two secretaries, a sort of younger one, and sort of older one. Farris Hotchkiss's office was next to mine.

Now I am not going to say I wasn't lonely. Girlfriend gone, classmates graduated, no more food at the Beta House, no more combo parties. Even though Terry was now in his senior year, I knew very few students and had not yet met any faculty or administrators. Yes, it was very lonely. The only thing to do was to throw myself into learning my new job. Farris and I talked a lot the first few weeks with his showing me the basics, his plans for the next few weeks and my formal training. We scheduled a trip for me to attend a five-day seminar for beginning development officers in Washington, D.C. in about 6 weeks. Since most of the money I would be raising was going to be from alumni, I spent a lot of time at the Alumni House at the end of the Colonnade, next to neighboring VMI and just up the road from the Beta House. We reviewed the next year's schedule of their trips to important Alumni chapters mostly around the Southeast and circled the ones I should join them on and make a speech (Gulp!). Since neither we nor the women's universities were yet in session, I took up my new weekend hobby of fly fishing (sort of) for trout in the mostly shallow rapids in the Maury River behind my house. Certainly convenient, lots of new equipment and paraphernalia to buy, and lots to learn. Never too sure of foot or athletic, I was fortunate not to have drowned. But as they say, even a blind squirrel finds an acorn every now and then, and even I eventually caught a few trout. Very exciting. I kept coming back for more.

In August, I went with the Alumni team to the Chicago Chapter but didn't have to give a speech. That night around midnight in my hotel room I watched Buzz Aldren land on the Moon on TV. Fascinating! The next week back in Lexington, I witnessed an event nearly as exciting and almost as historic. Hurricane Camille, in 36 hours, dropped a then record of 36 inches of rain on the Shenandoah Valley of Lexington, Virginia. I watched turtles cross the highway to reach higher ground. Afterwards I saw cows stranded in trees, and walked to the edge of a former Interstate highway and looked down more than 100 feet, where a former small stream cut a huge ravine. I learned nothing is more powerful than water in a hurry. Yes, Houston had an amazing 52 inches in 2017, but it was spread out over flatter land. What saved Lexington was the fact the storm broke on the top of the mountain, with half going down each side. Faster flowing water, but it did not stay around long. The Maury River rose to my back door, but then retreated.

In September the students returned, the girls' schools started up, and my pace quickened. I needed to publish a first- class fund raising brochure that would really make the alumni dig for their wallets before Christmas, so they could get their checks in the mail before year end to get their tax deduction. I read every W&L fund raising brochure written over the last ten years and took copious notes. After several weeks, I had prioritized the major points I wanted to make into a sequential outline. I knew the minimum and maximum number of words I could use and my most important goal. I began writing (in longhand). Before long the waste basket was overflowing! Trying too hard! Pulled my five best shots from the waste basket and started consolidating. Finally, it came together. I handed it to the junior secretary.

Having done that, I started thinking how I could make it a sexy, eye catching piece. Growing up, my parents had a subscription to "The New Yorker", and I reviewed them all, usually for the cartoons. I knew the regular contributors and I remembered one cartoon that had the right characters and attitude. I went to the bookstore and bought a couple of recent issues. Nothing. I went to the library and sure enough, they had every issue for the last ten years. I found several examples of his work and made copies, retrieved my typed copy of the brochure and made the final corrections. I took them all to Farris for his review, input and approval. We both approached our layout editor in the Journalism School and requested his input and ideas for an artist. He was fantastic. In two days we had the cartoon inserted into the copy. Bingo! Exactly what I was looking for! Eye catching, funny and pointed. Farris not only agreed—he was impressed! We got the final color copy on card stock, scored it for folding, ready for stuffing in an envelope and gave it to President Huntley and he approved it (not that we needed it). We printed all we needed along with self-addressed, postage paid pledge cards, hosted a stuffing party, and took them to the Alumni House for addressing and mailing. Mission accomplished and it wasn't even Thanksgiving yet!

This was clearly a confidence builder. I began putting the finishing touches on my speeches, practiced in front of the mirror and I was ready to hit the road. After the first of the year, the checks started rolling in on cue. We compared each week's total with the total from the same period in previous years. Each week we improved. I had time to squeeze in a couple of dates between trips out of town for alumni and parents meetings. While I was doing all this, Farris was working the "large donor" side of the house. He was doing better than last year as well. Now we were experiencing a relatively good economy and our constituency was pretty comfortable in the first place. They ought to be able to cough up a little more. Yes, these fund totals went up every year, seemingly on their own. But, we had clearly achieved better than average increases by the spring. I turned my attention quietly towards graduate school reapplications. Positive results occurred and I began to focus my attention on Emory University in Atlanta. I knew practically nothing about either, but each had a pretty good reputation. I finally accepted Emory's offer late in May, near their deadline. The parents arrived, Terry graduated with a job at a bank, admission to Law School at the University of Memphis, and his mind on matrimony to Karen Jones in his life from Jackson, Tennessee, fresh with a degree from Randolph Macon Women's College. Mother and Dad fell in love with her immediately.

Robin, the only brother qualified for military service, joined the U.S. Navy Reserves in Louisville, Kentucky; served honorably from 1968-1971, was on active duty from 1969-1971 aboard USS Wainwright (DLG-28) in southeast Asia/Vietnam. The Wainwright went around the world in service to this country during Robin's time aboard.

It is now the summer of 1971. Gwathmey married Varina Jefferson Davis Marret in April 1967 and lived in Anchorage. With the birth of Samuel Gwathmey Tyler IV in 1969, the notorious Tyler Dynasty had begun. Time for a visit to dear old Anchorage. My old friend Johnny Clark is marrying his long-time girlfriend, Gretchen Rounsavall of Louisville, June 19. On Friday night, Johnny and I are ready to leave his house at around 8 pm and his mother's last words were for us to have fun and not end up in jail. We were just going to join a few more of our friends at a strip club for a few drinks. How could we ever end up in jail? The first strip club was getting ready to close when we decided to go for just one more drink at an all-night joint in an even worse part of downtown. We headed off and I really wasn't sure where I was going when this other car with several thugs in it pulled up alongside us and started giving us some lip. The light turned green and we are racing side by side when they threw a beer bottle at me, shattering on my side-view mirror, showering me in beer and broken glass. I went berserk and after keeping up with them for a few blocks, they accelerated past us. The chase was on! We made turn after turn on two wheels, in a neighborhood that was getting worse and worse. They pulled into a driveway and when I pulled up, they were meeting with their friend on his front porch and they had a gun. About that time, the neighborhood turned blue, as a cop car pulled up behind me with siren blaring and a cop getting out of the car and started talking to the men on the porch like they knew one another. He came up to us and said, "You are coming downtown with us; get in the back of the car." We didn't realize it at the time, but they had just saved our lives. It was about 3 a.m. when I called Gwathmey and asked him to spring us. He said to call him back after they had booked us and hung up. There went my one phone call! Johnny called a friend of his and we settled into a cold, hard cell to get some sleep. They released us at about 7 a.m. Feeling like I had been run over by a truck, we retrieved my car from the police lot and went home to try to get a little more sleep. Needless to say, my toast at the wedding reception was probably the worst I had ever given.

  Back to the serenity of Lexington to resign and pack for Atlanta. I was sitting in Farris' office having just delivered the bad news, when President Bob Huntley walked in the room. Farris said that I was just telling him I was leaving, to which Bob Huntley responded, "Go to Hell!" Shocked and flabbergasted, I reached down for my fastest critical thinking and somehow blurted out, "Ugh, No, sir, it is Emory." Now I know the President had a big job to do, with a lot of money to raise and the last thing he needed was to replace someone he probably never wanted to hire in the first place, but I would be lying if I told you Bob Huntley did not drop several notches in my opinion with his comment. Afterward, Farris said he was surprised and angered by Bob's comment and not to let it bother me. He closed by stating I had been a big help to him and he would always give me a good recommendation. We are friends to this day. I left Lexington for good at the end of August.

EMORY BUSINESS SCHOOL

*A**tlanta is a big place.* Lots of things to see with lots of things to do. It was a great pick for a city. Now let's take a look at Emory. Emory was big too. Business School, Medical School, Law School, School of Divinity and others. Its Medical School was very highly ranked, but not so the Business School. The Finance side had a better reputation, but I was interested in Marketing. Again, I shied away from Finance because of statistics, calculus, etc., and favored Marketing because of my writing skills. I found a nearby, two bedroom apartment and a roommate and was ready to go.

    Graduate school was like undergraduate school in that if you had had the material before, you could coast through the first year. My friends from the W&L "C" School sailed right through year one. We Sociology and Journalism majors, not so much. Lots of classes, tons of reading. Somehow, I managed to avoid the library—maybe I had learned how to study or could lean more on critical thinking. A very interesting experience first year was my third turn at calculus. It was taught by a terrific professor trained at Harvard. He could teach calculus to a chimp. It was easy. Even I aced it! Talk about surprised and a big confidence builder, this was it. Although my grades in marketing were fine, I was bored for some reason. I never could put my finger on it. The little amount of finance and accounting I had first year, however, was fascinating and my grades showed it. To salvage the most out of my MBA, I decided to switch my "major" from Marketing to Finance the second year. Since I had to play catch up, I had to take more finance courses the second year and it was harder, but it was more interesting and my grades didn't suffer. To shake things up even further, I ditched my roommate and apartment over the summer and moved into a three-bedroom, two-bath house (the legendary 143 Mockingbird Lane) with two doctors. Let's be honest, this is when the fun began. One roommate was my old roommate and best friend, James Gilliam Burke. My second roommate was Bob Steele, from Chattanooga, Tennessee and graduate of The University of North Carolina at Chapel Hill. To this pair you could add the third best friend for the rest of my life, Arthur Hobart Warner from La Jolla, California, and graduated from the University of Virginia. He was married to Anne Bradford, an English major from Hollins College. He drove a scooter to and from class to class wearing an Army jacket he had earned in Vietnam.

The other two roommates in the house were Tuck, a wire-haired terrier belonging to Gil and Doc, a yellow Labrador belonging to Bob. Bob and Gil were studying to be orthopedic surgeons, interned together at Grady Hospital in Atlanta and later would practice together, Gil in Mt. Airy and Bob in Salisbury, North Carolina. Hoby and Anne and I spent the rest of our lives together in Atlanta as well. Bob had Gil's gift of genius, spending more time studying business than medicine. We partied and drank together all the time. On many a Saturday night we would get dates and play hide and go seek (yes, you read that correctly—mature graduate students). We would hide under beds, on the roof, in the bushes out front—nothing was off limits. On this particular night, there was ample drinking and Bob could not be found. We shouted that the game was over, he had won, we give up. Still no response, no Bob. We even watched TV a while, and then took our dates, and Bob's, home. The next morning, Gil and I were lounging around, reading the newspaper, when Bob walked sheepishly out of his bedroom. It turns out that Bob had crawled between his mattress and box spring, somehow covering himself back up with his bed spread and passed out due to a lack of oxygen, drunkeness or both. It was like this most of the time.

That second year flew by and before you knew it, spring had arrived and I would be needing a job soon. Head hunters and corporations were hanging around all spring. I signed up for every interview I could. One day the Dean said that I had made a good impression on Monsanto. He didn't do that very often, so I must have really made a good impression. If they chose me, they would fly me to their home office in St. Louis and I could see my parents. A month passed, then 6 weeks and finally the letter came addressed to WILBORN Tyler turning me down. The name stuck with me the rest of my life—humbling!

One corporation and I hit it off, by chance. A guy by the name of Mike Buchannon, a graduate of the University of Kentucky and I hit it off because of the Kentucky connection. He represented a company called CSRI, which was a subsidiary of C&S (short for Citizens and Southern or "Catch 'em and Squeeze 'em" (as they were affectionately called) Bank and C&S Mortgage Company. Since I would spend the rest of my career in this business, let's look at this more closely. CSRI was an REIT advised by the Citizen & Southern National Bank whose President was the legendary Georgia Banker Mills B. Lane. An REIT is a Real Estate Investment Trust, which raises its capital by selling shares on Wall Street and investing it in real estate. In CSRI's case, controlling shares were owned by C&S Bank and their subsidiary C&S Mortgage Company, formerly Atlantic Mortgage Company. Under the management contract between CSRI and C&S Bank, the officers of Atlantic Mortgage Company provided the management and investment advice to CSRI. CSRI was in the business of making land acquisition and construction loans to borrowers who built shopping centers, apartments, warehouses, and office buildings at 300 to 500 basis points over The Prime Rate of about 3%. CSRI used its stock to collateralize its internal loans at about 1 1/2% over The Prime Rate which is how it made a profit. Now all this made sense because Atlantic Mortgage Company was also in the business to make long term, fixed rate loans for terms of five to 30 years that paid off three to five-year construction loans. Then Atlantic Mortgage Company would sell their loans to Insurance Companies who had long term capital from the sale of life insurance policies. Atlantic Mortgage Company had represented many of these insurance companies for 20 to 30 years. REITs were invented by Wall Street firms in 1968 following the banking recession after which banks ceased making construction loans all together. As part of this legislation, the REITs were given two years after they raised the money to make the loans or they would be taxed prohibitively. That is why Mike came recruiting at Emory, was in a hurry, and was offering big salaries. That is why I went to work for him even though at the time I did not know what a REIT was. I was offered an annual salary of $18,000 (a 50% increase over W&L) in addition to a car allowance to work for the REIT, and I would report to the Bank and be paid by The Mortgage Company. If you think this smelled like a semi-legal, conflicted can of worms, you are likely correct, but all of Mills B. Lane's companies looked this way, and some thought they were a house of cards that would collapse at any time. Another troubling factor was the old adage that Wall Street has never known anything about banks and loans, and lenders have never known anything about Wall Street. To understand all this better, see Glass- Steagall Act. Due to all this rushed timing, there were about 12 to 15 of us MBAs hired from a half dozen MBA programs. We therefore acted like a fraternity pledge class and drank like one too. We were kings of the hill, were bonded, and had a fantastic time. About this time, my friend from W&L, Charlie Yates returned home to Atlanta, after a year of teaching history in New Orleans looking for a job and I sent him to Mike Buchannon. Why would I be interested in a job like this with a company like this? Lots of reasons. One of my main criteria for a career was one that did not demand geographic moves for advancement. I really didn't know much about real estate and felt this would be a good place to learn. I was a little familiar with banks having had a summer job at one. I knew I didn't want to be a banker. There is an old saying that if you stay at a bank for five years you will never leave. Thankfully, I would avoid that.

WORKING FOR CSRI

First a U.S. update. It is now the summer of 1973. My friend, Richard M. Nixon, was re-elected President of the U.S. in a landslide over George McGovern. The Watergate scandal is about to heat up. In the fall Atlanta would elect its first black mayor for three terms (12 years). He was 35, born in Dallas, Texas, educated at Morehouse College, Boston University Law and North Carolina Central Law. He was a Democrat, never worked a day in his life, was a gifted speaker (slick talker) whom everyone, including me, thought was finally the answer to race relations in Atlanta and the rest of the country. I believe he was the only Democrat I ever voted for. Big disappointment as were most.

The first several months at CSRI were orientation, education and then real work. It is important to know that the banker mentality controlled the entire process. First stop, Credit School, taught in the Credit department. Learn the five C's of credit—Character, Capacity, Capital, Collateral and Conditions; i.e. what makes a good loan and why. Next, off to a Bank Branch and learn what happens there, starting as a teller, cashing checks and hoping your window balances at the end of the day. (Tedious, more than you need to know.) Bankers really don't make much money and it takes forever to advance. In the overall scope of things real estate loans are not a big part of most banks' existence. Real estate loans are not meant to be made in the branches. Refer the client to the real estate department. The cycle of residential lending goes like this: A borrower wants to build a subdivision and needs a loan. He preferably has done this before and can pass the 5 C's of credit. The lender needs to know about land, construction and demand—each unique specialty. The loan is made with the borrower personally guaranteeing repayment and giving the property as additional collateral. If all goes well the homes are sold, repaying the loan. It becomes trickier when the borrower wants to build income producing property like an office building. These loans are much bigger (home costs $150,000; office building $15 million and take longer to build, plus lease fully (six months to a year for a house, three to five years for an office building). When up and leased, the mortgage must be repaid by a long- term mortgage (25 to 30 years.), typically from an insurance company, and in an amount equal to or greater than the current balance. It is said that a construction lender can be a borrower's best friend or mortal enemy. Why is that? If the lender for some reason refuses to fund. During the last financial crises, I had property 90% completed and 80% leased when the lender ran out of money. Nobody's fault, but the borrower lost everything he had. Basically, anything can go wrong and usually does. In 1973, in Atlanta, there were five construction loan REITS like CSRI all trying to throw money out the window at the same time, mostly for apartments. That year, combined, the five lenders funded the construction of 35,000 apartment units in Atlanta alone. At $20,000 per unit that totals $700,000,000 ($700 million). With a normal average annual rate of construction of 7,000 units a year that was a five-year supply, just for Atlanta. Each lender had no idea what the other was doing. Now multiply this times about five property types in at least a half-dozen cities, and you have a real mess brewing. As we said, lending money to developers was like giving whiskey to the Indians—they will take all they can get, and then some. With all this construction underway, eventually you run out of qualified sub-contractors, graders become framers, electricians become electrical engineers, plumbers become plumbing contractors and quality rapidly begins to decline. Eventually loans begin to default and REIT balance sheets begin to crumble. Sooner or later, Wall Street analysts begin to figure it out, stock values begin to fall, REITS can no longer sell new stock or issue fresh debt and the swirl towards the drain quickens. It was about this time that the cover of "Fortune Magazine" featured a pen and ink drawing of the entrance to the downtown Atlanta, C&S bank headquarters building with red ink spattered on it like blood. The article inside told the current saga, and the history of Mills B. Lane's twisted illegal corporate structures which were unraveling as CSRI would eventually make the bank fail. I knew the Art Editor of "Fortune Magazine", Ron Campbell as well as his wife Julie who initiated the first "Sports Illustrated" Swim Suit Edition and photo shot it every year. They were regulars at my old summer haunt, the Chalfonte Hotel. I called Ron and bought the original art work for the cover directly from the artist for $300. Well, no one else wanted it at the time, and it still hangs on my wall in my den, not far from my Dick Nixon calling card from Berlin.

Meanwhile, back at the office, I had finished my bank training and was running around the REIT offices in the "Round Building" at North Avenue and West Peachtree asking questions about real estate lending. The "Round Building" was interesting since it was built from the top down. A giant 20-story concrete core column was erected and then each floor was "hung" on the column. The stairwells, elevators and restrooms were in the core and offices on the outside, all wrapped in glass and bronzed aluminum. Neat, but a bear to heat and cool comfortably. In the hay day, the loan officers would board C&S flown helicopters on the roof to go inspect properties. These were the same helicopters the Bank used to hook satchels of checks and other paperwork hoisted atop Polls at each branch and brought to a central location, avoiding Atlanta's traffic snarls. The original C&S "hooker," who hung out of the chopper snagging satchels was a good friend. This was just another soon-to-be-infamous folly of Mills B. Lane. The question I had asked of Jim Field, Vice President of Production, could only be answered in his estimation, by the one and only father of Atlantic Mortgage Company and CSRI, Mr. Ed Reeves. I found him safely hidden in his office which would have been a corner office, but a round building doesn't have any. When I asked him my question, he thought for a minute and then uttered prolific advice I have always remembered, "Bill, sometimes I feel like the whole world is being run on hurt feelings." What he was speaking of then was almost the same as it is now, but updated. In the mid 1960's the banks crashed; made all the borrowers mad; Congress tried to solve it with the REIT law and now here we are again in the mid 1970s about to crash it again. Nobody intended it. Ed Reeves was a founder and principal of Atlantic Mortgage, which the bank bought for nothing and then demoted him to be a lending officer at CSRI. Nobody intended it. Dick Nixon was being hounded by everybody for Watergate. Nobody intended it. The Vietnam War started in 1955 and would not end until 1975. Nobody intended it. Martin Luther King died in 1968, but black unemployment remained at high levels. Nobody intended it. All of the insurance companies with whom Mr. Reeves placed loans in the 1950's and 1960's saw those loans crumbling with the REIT overbuilding and they were mad that he and all his employees had quit courting them and were feeding the REITS. But again, nobody intended it. You can probably draw the parallels with today's economic, political and global wars, race relations and real estate conditions. Nobody intended it!

After about six months of my making CSRI loans, Jim Field could see it coming to an end and sent me to the Mortgage Company to try to repair Life Insurance Company relationships. I was the new boy to them. Obviously green and untrained, I probably couldn't do it any worse than my predecessors. Did they have hurt feelings? Oh yeah. Did they let me know it? Sure. I was not impressed with who they had left in charge, nor was Field. I begged him to reassign him somewhere else so I could take charge. Eventually, after my predecessor introduced me to all the lenders at the annual National Mortgage Bankers Convention, they let me run it. Now it was about 1974. One day I stepped onto a nearly empty elevator next to an attractive new trainee and in a low voice introduced myself rather boldly, "My name is Bill Tyler and I am single." She responded coldly, "I am Beth and I am not." Undeterred, I asked her later to go to dinner. She was single, but felt in need of more protection. Now dating someone where you work is seriously frowned upon if not prohibited. This was tricky and risky. Emotional lover spats at work would not be permitted. Dating a person who works for you was likely illegal and would not be permitted. Our interpretation and testimony would be that she administered loans in the

REIT for someone else and I worked for a different company, the mortgage company. Amazingly, they both had the same name. Both of us had our friends and admirers who would stick by us in a pinch. We tried to tell as few people as possible and only on a need to know basis. Our first date was memorable, more for her than me. Dinner was fine and I signaled the waiter to bring me the check. It finally arrived. I put my credit card with it and signaled the waiter again and eventually he took it away. We waited five minutes. After ten minutes, I stood up, told Beth we were leaving, and headed to the door. Outside, she put her hands on her hips and demanded to know What the Hell I was doing. I simply replied that we were going to the car, and when they noticed, they would bring my card. We were in the car, backing out of the space when the waiter came running out shouting and demanding we re-enter the restaurant with him. I re-parked the car and followed him inside. I asked him where my check was. He walked away to get it and I waited about three more minutes and I left again pulling Beth. He caught us quicker this time. I took my card, crossed off any tip, signed it and scratched off, leaving the lot. Yes, I am very impatient when it comes to waiting for service. Over the years we did this several times and Beth finally got used to it.

Bob Steele and Gil Burke graduated from Medical School that summer and headed off to the Carolinas for their Surgical Residency. They cleared out about everything from old 143 Mockingbird Lane. Doc, Tuck, pots, pans, their bedroom furniture and the TV. I bought the big stuff, couches and a few chairs for cents on the dollar. They hadn't been gone two days when I came down with a cold, nagging cough and a sore throat. The doc said it was walking pneumonia and he could check me into the hospital or send me home with strong meds. I chose home, thinking I could get some girlfriend to move in and take care of me. No luck; got weaker and weaker, nothing to eat or cook anything in. Finding myself too feeble to get up and walk around, I called Anne and Hoby Warner begging for cooked food. They dropped off a hot prepared dinner, groceries, pots and pans that afternoon. In about a week, I crawled back to work, half well, but no longer contagious. Hating the hassle of moving, I bought the old house from the owner, Opal Phoenix. I got a good price, figured I wouldn't live there too long and could always get my money out because of the location. I borrowed about 100% of cost from C&S Bank, closed my first ever real estate loan and purchase and never looked back. By about this time, the house next door was purchased by a CSRI co-worker and his wife. He previously was a very successful computer salesman for IBM. They kept cutting back his territory and upping his quota, so he quit and came seeking his next fortune at CSRI. Beth lived in an apartment less than a mile away and we started seeing more and more of each other. Before long we were doing home and away sleep-overs, leaving late at night or early in the morning. Our theme song became Simon & Garfunkel's "Sounds of Silence"—Hello darkness my old friend. But we could keep neighbor Rob in the dark just so long. One day he asked me quietly if Beth and I were dating. I nodded, he gave me the thumbs up and zipped lip signs and never said a word. Rob and his wife and Beth and I had some great times. Our most memorable was a trip to a local night club where the popular singing group, The Shirelles, performed live. Supported by ample libations, and pushed on stage by my evil friends, I found myself on stage, microphone in hand, gyrating with the trio loudly singing, "Will you still love me tomorrow?" Critical thinking: don't quit your day job!

For some reason the Tyler men picked this time to get the Resort Retirement Real Estate Investment disease and since I was the real estate guru and Dad had all the money, we were in charge of picking beach or mountain, location, and making sure we could afford it. After one trip to Savannah, we knew the beach was too expensive and after one stop in the North Carolina Mountains, we quickly decided on the North Georgia Mountains. The location was really pretty good—about a six-hour drive from Louisville, five from Greensboro and an hour north of Atlanta. Out of two choices we decided on Big Canoe, a joint venture between Tom Cousins, an Atlanta developer, and The Sea Pines Company at Hilton Head. Amenities featured a scenic lake, an 18-hole golf course, club house and restaurant. We chose a cheap wooded lot with not much view, but it provided golf privileges. We closed on ten-year financing at closing under my name and we would split the monthly payment and association fees five ways. A week after closing I took a date up there to show it off. As we entered the front gate the guard greeted us with, "Welcome to Big Canoe, Mr. Tyler. Enjoy your stay!" When I was bragging to my friend, Hoby Warner, a few weeks later he scoffed that the greeting was no big surprise to him since everyone knew that the only people that owned property at Big Canoe were me and Tom Cousins.

Tyler Clan at Big Canoe

THE MASTERS IN AUGUSTA

When *you are selling* yourself as a real estate finance wizard to both lenders and borrower/developers, you need to entertain them both and entertain them royally. The Masters Tournament in Augusta, the first weekend after the first full week in April, is the finest place you can be for just that. The azaleas are guaranteed to be at their peak and the beauty of the lady patrons in their spring finery is matched only by the quality of the golf. With tickets scarce as hens' teeth, four days and nights of 100% selling, an unlimited budget for food and drink and plenty of exercise and sunshine walking the course, The Master's is unbeatable for making lasting relationships and big deal sales. My W&L friend Charlie Yates' father played golf with the legendary champion Bobby Jones, who founded Augusta National Golf Club and the Master's Tournament. Big Charlie was a founding member of Augusta National and was honored every year by staying in the Butler Cabin on the 18th hole, where the coveted Green Jacket is awarded to the Tournament Champion on Sunday afternoon. Charlie could get almost an unlimited number of tickets, badges and passes each year and CSRI knew this was their Number One sales event each year. As such, they funded the weekend rental houses where we stayed; the food; liquor; and made the entire fleet of the C&S fixed wing turbo prop aircraft available to shuttle all our guests to and from Augusta each day. And who was put in charge of arranging and hosting all this? Me and Charlie. It was nasty work, but somebody had to do it! They didn't teach me this at Emory, but my Dad sure did! Charlie and I had more friends than you could shake a stick at on those weekends, and Charlie was run ragged with requests throughout the year. With Charlie in charge of ticket procurement, I, of course was in charge of everything else. I didn't mind because it was for a worthy cause—Me! Beth started joining me over there every year on the weekend and was a big help. Yes, we ran into the CSRI big wigs every now and then, but since it was a day time, business type thing, no one put two and two together.

BETH AND I GET MARRIED

Having gone to one National Mortgage Bankers' five-day convention, I realized the need to go every year starting with golf with lenders on Saturday and Sunday, followed by lender meetings on Monday, Tuesday, and a half day on Wednesday. It tended to rotate every year between Orlando and San Diego. Later got to go to Chicago, Boston, New York City and even Atlanta. We also got to meet competing Mortgage Brokers and Bankers around the country. A big-name producer was Coldwell Banker with multiple offices in California. They even brought some California developers to develop shopping centers with CSRI in Atlanta and other eastern cities. Coldwell Banker opened its first real estate office in 1906 in San Francisco, California after the earthquake. They began moving east in the mid '60's and opened in Atlanta in 1972, bought local residential company Barton and Ludwig in 1973, and held their annual meeting here in 1975. Back at CSRI, by this time I was making good money, and Beth and I decided to get married. After getting corporate approval, we began telling close friends and associates. No one was really surprised. We were both ready. I was 29, the only unwed brother and Beth was 25. My parents came to town bearing Edmonia's wedding ring and met Beth and her parents, which went very well. We set the date for an engagement party in April and wedding date for October 30, Beth's 25th birthday. Then I called all the brothers and told them to plan trips to Atlanta for April and October. Before long the schedules got busier and the pressure mounted. We designed the setting for the engagement ring and ordered wedding bands. We met with the Presbyterian Church to set the date and time and met with the minister. We picked out invitations for the engagement party, and wedding and invitees for each. We decided on the members of the wedding party, booked the Piedmont Driving Club for the rehearsal dinner through a W&L friend, and the Ansley Golf Club for the wedding reception through Beth's Uncle Joe. Beth registered us for gifts and I met with real estate agents about selling my house and finding a new one. In my spare time, I booked flights and five days free at a house in a secure compound outside of Montego Bay in Jamaica for our honeymoon. Somewhere in here I did some real estate deals. Beth and I looked at houses, concentrating on the Morningside area where a lot of young couples were gentrifying neighborhoods. We began circling a house in an estate with a bullet hole in the red front door, owned by a pharmacist and his wife, a French heiress, who collected art, riddling the plaster walls with holes in every room. She died in the house of an overdose of drugs and alcohol; and he, turning gay, married his boyfriend selling off the paintings to enhance their lifestyle. He eventually killed himself, also in the house, or was killed by his lover, as later learned by the brother of the deceased owner in a seance held in the house. Now you would think that with two deaths in the house it would be way too creepy to attract too many bidders and I would therefore get a decent price.

It was almost too creepy for Beth! I put it under contract and arranged for another loan at C&S Bank. We toured the home several times during the inspection period. One bedroom upstairs with ugly shag carpeting and mirrors on the ceiling, plus a bathroom and nursery, two bedrooms downstairs with a den, living room, dining room, breakfast room, kitchen, basement with washer, dryer connections and wet bar. Outside, a walled off slate patio, small grassy area and a two-car garage. We were told by the agent not to open the refrigerator door because it had never been opened since the owner died. Finally, I couldn't stand it any longer, opened it quickly, saw some jars and unopened containers and slammed it back shut. Looked great to me. After we closed on the sale, I opened it up again. Everything was almost totally black, covered in mold. Mold can't grow without oxygen. I eventually emptied and cleaned it thoroughly, loaded it with charcoal, shut it for another week and it was very serviceable. Yes, I AM a cheap SOB. The house closed and two days later we got married. We said our I do's at North Avenue Presbyterian church at 5 p.m. At 6:00, I was greeted at The

Ansley Golf Club with, "Congratulations, Mr. Tyler, your club membership has been approved." The initiation fee was $100 and Aunt Sally and Uncle Joe got a free dinner out of it. This now meant Dad could charge his scotch and waters at the bar instead of drinking champagne, which he hated. It was a welcome surprise to a memorable evening. Then off to Jamaica the next day and back to work the next Monday.

Dick Nixon resigned after Watergate and Gerald Ford moved into the White House. In the 1976 Presidential election Ford ran against Jimmy Carter, former Governor of Georgia. My CBRE colleagues across the U.S. wanted to know what I thought of him. I said I wouldn't vote for him for dogcatcher. In return I asked my California colleagues, about their governor, Jerry Brown, who was also seeking the nomination. They responded the same as I had for Carter. I was happy to see all the Republicans in CBRE, but not so happy when Carter won.

WORKING FOR CBRE

CBRE *started adding* mortgage operations to their commercial offices in 1977, and I opened the Atlanta office for the Southeast on the same day friend Charlie O'Donnell opened up his operation in Hackensack, New Jersey, and friend, Mike Richwine in Oakbrook (Chicago), Illinois. We had all been hired about the same time, and all had met with the CBRE "shrink" in San Francisco, California. He gave us all a test that was looking for "sitability". Executing a commercial real estate finance transaction on average takes longer than a sale, lease or just about any other type real estate transaction. First you must get hired; then analyze the transaction and build a presentation; then take it to market, negotiate the terms with each potential finance source; get it approved by the winner; accepted by the borrower; closed, and paid. To be successful, you need to have many deals in process at all times. It is like having 25 fishing lines in the water at once, constantly hooking fish, fighting with them, landing them, killing, cleaning, cooking and finally eating them. That is "sitability." You have to be highly motivated, trained and paid. A company simply cannot afford high turnover and must provide ever changing tools required to close deals. In addition to a salary, a producer is paid a commission on each closing, the percentage of which grows the more a producer closes in each year. Since the business is always in flux, these percentages change annually. If the company gets too greedy, producers leave—sometimes in droves. Finally, to grow an office and a national company, head producers need to hire, manage, and train a staff, analysts and junior producers, plus produce their own book of business. I was lucky enough to bring Mike Doll and Charlie Yates with me from CSRI and hire the son of a lender who had just graduated from college as a trainee/analyst shortly after opening the office. Business began to grow and we hired more staff. Times were good.

Now is a good time to revisit the critical thinking involved in my decision to stay in Atlanta for what became the rest of my life. By this time Gwathmey had added three sons, and Terry had two sons and a daughter, all of whom lived in Louisville. Looks like they had sewn up that location. Robin had two sons living in Greensboro, North Carolina. No reason to go there either. Beth, however, had spent her whole life in Atlanta and had a lot of friends here. Bingo, Atlanta! Now all the other reasons. It was the capital of the south and its largest city. It had the busiest airport in the world with direct flights to anyplace you might want in the world. It had plenty of colleges and universities of every type. It had pro teams in every major sport and arenas for each. It had entertainment venues of all sorts and sizes. There were ample sports venues from rafting on the Chattahoochee River to kite flying in Piedmont park, to public and private golf courses galore. It was the second highest city in the nation (behind Denver), plenty of rainfall and four distinct seasons. Secondary schools were poor to average at best, but there were plenty of good private schools if you had the connections and money. It had the largest percentage of black residents of any city in the country and a black mayor. The only negatives that persist for Atlanta are consistently heavy traffic and the occasional crippling ice storm: For all these reasons and more it attracted plenty of jobs, corporations and corporate headquarters. With all this commercial activity, there was a growing demand for commercial real estate finance, and CBRE and I were the ones to provide it.

Although not totally related, critical thinking is important to what sort of company is the best for ownership in a real estate finance business. The big word here would have to be sustainability. I think out of necessity, finding the right ownership has to be by trial and error. Let's start with a bank. Two major problems here—capital and management greed. If you run out of capital to lend, by definition, you are not sustainable. The bank mentality of management greed consistently leads to employee turnover and unsustainability. Senior management simply will not pay a lowly loan production whore more than anyone in senior management. Left C&S Bank and CSRI. Consider a sole proprietorship option. One thing about the business we have not yet fully explained is the insurance company lenders' remedy for sustainability. When you place financing with an insurance company, compensation is split between a transaction fee and a servicing fee. The servicing fee is paid every year to the "correspondent" for collecting the monthly mortgage payments from the borrowers and for sustaining that company through the recessions when life companies don't make loans. These servicing fees build up over time and are the primary creators of value for correspondents. Companies are bought and sold solely based on these values. In periods of high earnings volatility in recent decades, these correspondents have proven to be unsustainable. A sole proprietorship operating under this model is particularly vulnerable. Now let's move to the other end of the spectrum to the CBRE model that creates a blend huge geographic diversity and size with huge diversity in the sources of revenue. Today CBRE has operations all over the globe and hundreds of sources of revenue types, almost too many to mention including every imaginable property type; i.e. from office to apartments and property sales to property management to leasing. It is a very slick model, but it took decades to build and there was plenty of carnage along the way. Just wait and see.

CBRE opened their offices in Downtown Atlanta in Peachtree Center. My five person finance division was across the hall from the 25-person sales and leasing office and next to a four-person property management division. Each division loosely shared revenues with the other. Property management people were paid 100% salary; sales and leasing, 100% commission; finance, a mysterious blend of salary plus commission that was ever changing. We all reported to the local sales manager, but each division reported up a different chain of command located in Houston and Los Angeles. All went swimmingly for a while. To some extent we shared clients, cordially. The sales side reported up to a regional head out of Houston—James Didion. He was responsible for opening all the offices outside of Los Angeles, had an ego to match his growing territory and rarely smiled when he came to town. I remember one day when he walked into the office; a successful apartment broker who played plenty of golf, stood in his cube and yelled, "Hey Jim, you wanna' play some golf while you are in town?" Without smiling Jim responded, "I don't play golf with salesmen on draw!" To which the salesman smiled "If I played with you, I wouldn't need to be on draw."

Jim didn't run the finance department and did not like anyone in it. We stayed out of each other's way.

Times were generally good and we were making good money. One day at the Masters there was a rain delay, and I asked a guest of Charlie Yates' from California, Jim Griggs, what he did (for a living). He said he was in the real estate investment advisory business and his largest client wanted to grow their investments out of California into the east. We asked him who his client was and he said The California Public Employees Retirement System and added that he was their sole advisor in real estate investments but not doing much business out of California himself, he wasn't sure how to advise or help them. CALPERS, as they were called, were the largest public retirement investment firm in the country and had billions invested in stocks and bonds, but pennies in real estate, and all in California. The rating agencies were telling them they needed to diversify outside of California. Charlie and I about fell out of the golf cart.

This was huge, but how could we capitalize on it? In a few weeks, it dawned on us—we needed to start our own company and advise CALPERS in the Southeast. More easily said than done. I have already told you that a diversified company beats the hell out of a sole proprietorship, but it was beginning to look like the California earthquake would shake the profits out of CBRE and we would have no better option. By now it was 1978 and we were in another financial crisis. Good old President Jimmy Carter had driven inflation through the roof and interest rates with it—both were above 18%. Lending stopped cold. If real estate values increased as fast as interest rates, the best place to be would be in unlevered real estate. No one wanted to loan--everyone wanted to own. But banks and insurance companies, by law, couldn't own real estate. Change the laws and through smoke and mirrors make debt act like equity or ownership. Enter a new beginning— structured real estate finance. The brokerage boys didn't know what happened to them. They didn't know financial institutions or how to structure a deal with them if they did know them. We real estate finance guys started doing most of the deals and to keep management happy, we would tap some sales guy on the shoulder at closing, hand him a check for a $100,000 and wish him Merry Christmas. Well it didn't take Didion long to figure it out and go running to senior management screaming that the finance guys, particularly Tyler, were stealing all the money from the sales guys. We finance producers knew it was financing and we deserved the fee; they (management) said it was a sales commission and they were due all the fee. The brokers still had no clue what was going on. The finance guys knew that if we gave away the fee, we would die immediately, and if we split it 50-50, we would die tomorrow. Didion insisted that the board of directors needed to make the decision. We knew who ran what and we were about to get screwed. Most of us turned up the heat on old Plan B. In a few weeks our old friend management greed showed up and they decided to split the fee, no matter who did the work. Brokers still had no clue meaning we would do all the work and they would take half the fee. Within a month, a dozen finance guys would leave—hell, five of us including staff were in Atlanta. Smelling blood in the water, another dozen around the country would leave the next month. About the time I resigned, there was a going away party for Jim Didion who was going back to Houston. At the cocktail party, I made it a point to tell Jim that I hoped he would bury the hatchet knowing our paths would likely cross again. He said, and I quote, "Bill, go f—k yourself!" Obviously, I needed to work on my exits after this and W&L.

TYLER YATES FINANCIAL GROUP

After a while, if you use good critical thinking you can smell where this business is going and plan accordingly. By the time I resigned, CBRE had moved to The Galleria 100 Building on Atlanta's Perimeter, developed by W&L graduate (are you keeping count?) Don Childress. I asked him to build out some generic space as he developed the 200 building and I would make sure he didn't lose money even if we didn't take it. Sure enough, we didn't even need a moving van. We hired an attorney, a marketing consultant, wrote a brochure, bought furniture and art work with the help of an interior decorator, found an accountant and a business partner. We had hired a young Duke graduate as an analyst, Elizabeth Honey, and along the way met her Dad, Kim and his wife Anne from Richmond, Virginia. He was a developer; his brother lived in Atlanta and he wanted us to finance his project. Having just been married and never run my own business, I was scared of not making payroll and really wanted a backstop. Kim agreed, put up a few dollars with a promise for more if we really needed it. I knew what the cost of running an office was, but also knew that no one can accurately project revenue. I agreed to be Chairman, Charlie took President and, since T comes before Y, we executed a partnership agreement and opened the doors to Tyler Yates Financial Group. As I mentioned before, we were in a financial recession and our business was structured finance. We had kind of a niche in this new kind of financing already, and since our established competitors were primarily in the old life company mode, we had a head start. Our first stop was to help Jim Griggs and CALPERS. Tyler Yates Financial Group was born in 1984.

CUMSTOUN AND THE MAITLAND FAMILY IN SCOTLAND

B*ut first, Beth and I* were headed to France, London and Scotland. Having just started my own company, almost the last thing I wanted to do was go to Europe. But boy am I glad we did. Dad had raved about our distant second cousins for a long time. Gwathmey had been to see them several years ago when he and Nina were across the pond, and he raved about them as well. Since everybody has been to France and England, let's go straight to Scotland. Having toured London for several days, we rented a car and headed north, on the wrong side of the road. Now getting used to that takes a lot of critical thinking and some horn blowing as well! After stopping for directions just outside of Kirkudbright, we headed to Cumstoun. When I first saw Cumstoun, the castle, it took my breath away even though I had seen pictures. Looming three stories and features 19 bedrooms, almost the same number of fireplaces, a giant great room, separate dining room, kitchen and owner's ground floor apartment with sitting room and bathroom. A grand staircase ascends to the second and third stories. Most of the frequently used guest rooms and baths are on the second floor, including the one with the famous hugging bed severely sloped to the middle after centuries of use.

We were met at the door by Adam and Hopi Maitland, his wife and our cousin, and their springer spaniel, Cobber; and were immediately offered tea as four pm was approaching. After a quick tour of the dining room, kitchen and owners' sitting room and apartment, we nestled into overstuffed couches on either side of a burning fire in the great room fireplace sipping our tea. It was like we had known Hopi and Adam all our lives. They were both on the short side, he with gray hair and moustache, she with dark brown hair and stout figure. He had retired from a printing company in London years ago. They had six children, Sarah, the eldest and noted liberal leaning author Coogie refused to read; David, second, who worked in London as a printer; Jamie, third; Robert who ran the 2,000 acre farm on the property and lived in a cottage on the place with his wife; Frippe, who lived in St. Andrews with her husband and ran a bed and breakfast; and lastly Maggie. After tea we took our bags up the stairs to our hugging bed and came downstairs to join Adam and Hopi for several scotches and wine as we prepared dinner, caught them up on news from my family, and planned the next few days' agenda. Then off to bed for a warm slumber under a heavy duvet in the hugging bed. The next day we marveled at the immaculate grass tennis court and surrounding grounds, including a number of cottages for family and farm workers. We went to the dairy for a quart of freshly squeezed milk and fresh eggs. After a quick lunch we headed out for an afternoon hike which included a look at a marker commemorating the Bessemer steel-making process. The return hike was more downhill which we welcomed, but when we spotted Cumstoun, it appeared there was smoke rising from a chimney which seemed unusual. But Adam seemed to sense one thing more and quickened his pace. Hopi volunteered that she had hoped to have a longer outing, but it looked like we had better follow Adam. When we arrived, Adam was already making repairs. It seems that they had a plumber come three days ago to fix a leak on the third floor, and it had taken three days to prove he had failed. Adam had stopped the flow of water falling from the ceiling and the mop up and carpet roll-back was in progress. We started to help, when Hopi demanded we stop because it was now 4:00 p.m. and nothing stops four-o'clock tea in Scotland. While enjoying our tea, I asked where the Maitland plaid was, so, I could get a kilt made. She admonished me rather boldly that the Maitlands did NOT wear dresses which were reserved for the highlanders who were sheep and goat herders. The Maitlands were proud lowlanders who farmed for a living. She was really downright disappointed that I was so stupid about such things. I chose not to tell her that the proper response from a Scot when queried what is worn under a kilt is "well, nothing at all. Everything is kept in perfect order!" We had to leave the next day, but if we had started our trip with Hopi and Adam, we would never have seen the rest of Europe on our scheduled trip.

"MAY DAY, MAY DAY! DOG HOUSE ONE? THIS IS DOG HOUSE TWO!"

I*t was a good thing* we decided to go to Europe before having children, because, sure enough, our daughter, Margaret Moffatt, was born January 22, 1980. Beth would end up staying home for 10 years before getting a full-time job because we could afford to do it. Basically, we caught another wave. Jim Griggs and CALPERS were the real deal. They appreciated our diligent research and heeded our advice. Too many investors think they know it all. In truth, our position in the market allows us to see things that no single investor can see on his own. With this kind of lender rapport, we are able to attract quality developers with multiple quality deals. Plus having the ability and growing success allows us to brag on that success with other investors, catch that next wave, and do it all over again. CALPERS' first deal was a joint venture with a seasoned developer on a "spec" (unleased) office building on the central perimeter, with no immediate access to a full interchange with the Interstate. A major factor in our selling that deal was using my critical thinking, imagination and luck, to video record the dynamics of the building and location from a helicopter, which had never been done in our market previously. It was a much easier sell with that perspective (done all the time today with drones). The next wave was even a trickier high wire attempt without a net. My friend, associate and former employee, Mike Doll, had graduated into the development business by then and successfully put a piece of land under contract in Buckhead others had mistakenly bypassed and was discussing the transaction with a major tenant to pre-lease half of the building. He needed not only a construction loan, but also an equity partner. Even with a substantial pre-lease, this was a tall order for a novice developer, with very little equity, net worth or development experience. Since we knew Mike so well and trusted him, we took a chance. Our long equity search finally led us to a billionaire named Henry Hillman in Pittsburgh, Pennsylvania, advised by an old acquaintance of mine whom I had met when he did deals for Aetna. Because of Mike's limitations, Hillman was advised to require that Mike get a construction loan prior to committing, and just to make it next to impossible to do, it must be non-recourse which was unheard of at the time. We then initiated an even longer search for a non-recourse construction loan. That road finally took us to Mellon Bank, Hillman's lead bank in Pittsburgh, which none of us knew and really did not make many construction loans even to Hillman. Finally, we got them to fund the land purchase, only to hear the next day that they had not gotten it approved and were withdrawing their funds. Thanks to the quick work of Doll's attorney, my good everlasting friend who is the smartest real estate attorney in the business, Charlie Sharbaugh, had already grabbed the funds and funded the land loan. Too late—we had to move forward.

During this time Doll, Sharbaugh and I were working together all the time. Doll and I would go out many a night way too late drinking. One night, imbued with too much alcohol and way too many war movies, in the dog house myself, I called the Doll house at 1:30 a.m. Mike's attractive and hilarious wife, Kate, answered the phone. Picturing the scene at their house and the sermon Mike was likely suffering, I blurted, "May Day! May Day! Dog House One, this is Dog house Two!" She burst out laughing and handed the phone to Mike. Mission accomplished!

ONLY THE PIZZA MAN GETS PAID

By this time, we had sunk about 18 months of spec time into this deal—Capital City Plaza. Mike Doll was about broke, had quit paying his phone bill (and any other bill he could get away with), made and took all his calls at Charlie Sharbaugh's law office and because we were there every night late working for a month, we ate pizza there every night and Doll even slept there half the time. To lighten things up, I declared that the name of my first real estate book was "Only the Pizza Man gets Paid." About a month earlier, Mike's mother had died and he was driving her un-plated car across town to his house and was stopped by a policeman and given a citation. He forgot about it, didn't pay it, the police came to his house, cuffed him and hauled him off to jail to the horror of his children and his great embarrassment and protest. He called his wife, Kate, and confessed he had no money to get out of jail and suggested she try to get it from a neighbor and come get him out. She arrived at the jail, threw down the cash and served him divorce papers. Not his finest hour. From here things got even worse. There were cost overruns, leasing was slow, Mellon dodged funding any money they didn't absolutely have to. Sharbaugh kept holding their feet to the fire. Once the building was finished, we felt obliged to move our offices there. It was a beautiful building, inside and out and we spared no expense making our space top of the line. The building did not lease sufficiently during construction, so a permanent loan could not be found and the construction loan had to be extended incurring more fees to Mellon bank and more interest carry. Long story short, Mike's interest in the development dwindled to zero. Mike, however, has incredible internal fortitude. Being a strong Notre Dame Catholic, he began attending daily Mass and moved in with his daughters. He needed to restart his life and career. We welcomed him back to work with us. We had very little salary to offer him, but he was welcome to any commissions he earned. In September 1990, the Atlanta miracle occurred when it was announced that our fair city had won the 1996 Summer Olympic Games. They had been held in the U.S. only three times previously—twice in Los Angeles and once in St. Louis. Billy Payne was credited with the win along with the help of hundreds. Now could we pull it off without going bankrupt? Charlie decided it would be a great PR move for TYFG to win the RFP for the Olympic Village which had been promised for a site adjacent to Georgia Tech in Midtown. We got busy. After putting together a number of charrettes to vet many potential team members, we picked a team of 24 members who were qualified by the Olympic committee. It was an incredibly diverse group of black and female owned companies as had been requested. Low and behold we won the bid. Charlie and I agreed that the Olympics would be great for Atlanta, but not everybody agreed. Nevertheless, we needed to divide and conquer-I would refocus on production and he could remain focused on the Olympics.

It might be helpful if we paused here and review what is going on in the rest of the country and what impact it might have on Atlanta. After ruining the economy by increasing inflation and interest rates to 18%, and, unable to get over 40 hostages released from Iran, Jimmy Carter lost to Ronald Reagan and George H.W. Bush in 1980. After getting the hostages released the day he was inaugurated, lowering taxes and restoring the economy, Reagan was reelected over Walter Mondale in 1984. In 1988, Bush continued the prosperity parade by defeating Michael Dukakis. Four years later in 1992 the parade not only ended, but the air was let out of the balloon when Bush lost to William Jefferson Blythe Clinton III. Atlanta, the capital of the southeast, continued to prosper over the period and the Olympic announcement enhanced its image but not its real estate market. The longer Clinton was in the White House, the more she began to sputter. By 1994, her propeller had stopped and she was gliding toward a safe but bumpy landing for her Olympic debut.

THE TYLER DYNASTY GROWS

T**he Tyler family during this** period grew when son Will was born March 30, 1983, and we moved to toney, high tax, Buckhead shortly thereafter, just off prominent West Paces Ferry in the upscale Private School district. I vowed after my disastrous freshman Year at W&L that my children, if at all possible, would get a quality private school education, no matter what it cost. Furthermore, I would try everything I could to avoid sending them to lower and middle public school (cheaper option if failed to get accepted at Privates), because entry into the Privates was four times as difficult at that level and educationally, a mid-course correction from the unprepared Public to the rigorous Private regimen is just asking for trouble. That fall, we toured and Meg applied to the four most highly ranked private schools in the area. As we mentioned earlier, one of Atlanta's problems was its public-school systems, especially in the city proper which was primarily a poor black demographic with a series of corrupt black mayors. This meant that the private schools could charge whatever they wanted and their waiting lists got longer and longer the more Atlanta grew. The sole bright spots were the public lower and middle schools that were full of a rich white demographic that had been unable to get into the private schools. Meg was now 13, had done well in lower school and tested well. She at least had a shot. We called all the board members we could find at all four schools, went over Meg's credentials and pedigree with them to assure them she would make them a star and prayed. Finally, the heads of admission were requiring us to tell them what school we would pick if admitted. We narrowed it to Pace Academy which was practically next door and ranked fourth in most applicants' opinion and number one, Westminster, almost next door in the other direction. If we didn't get into Westminster we would likely go to Pace. We got into Pace and Lovett. We turned to ANOTHER W&L Graduate Neely Young, Assistant Headmaster at Pace, to insure at the end of the day we would attend. The schools hated to go to their wait list of acceptances if rejected by another acceptee. At last, a match! We started in the Fall. Now how do I pay for it all?! I ended up paying for 13 years of tuition for both Meg and Will totaling about $500,000! And for those of you keeping score at home, after son Will was counted, the Tyler Dynasty totaled 15 and the score was Boys 12 (80%)-Girls 3(20%) over 41 years (remember spouses don't count in Tyler land). In just 34 more years the total will nearly double and the score will be Boys 20(69%)-Girls 9(31%)—a 75% increase for the Boys, but a 300% increase for the Girls.

As in all families every now and then, there is bad news, and this time ours came in bunches. In 1979, just before Meg was born, Mom and Dad moved to the Sea Pines Plantation on Hilton Head Island in South Carolina. It was a great spot for them—they knew some old WW II friends before they moved, Dad played golf and there was a 5:00 cocktail party every afternoon with more friends. Dad would rent a house for us and most of us found our way there for a week every year. Sadly, Dad died of a stroke on October 2, 1985. Mom died in Louisville on April 10, 1991. Now I am the first to admit that I do not do well at funerals, especially for those I know well, like my parents. But Mom's funeral was particularly tough. Mother was godmother to Cappy Cohen, because Mother had given Cappy's mother blood to save her life when Cappy was born. Cappy had become an Episcopal priest, above Mom's protest as a traditionalist. So Cappy came to the brothers and asked if she could give Mom's eulogy. We had to huddle on that one. We knew Mom would likely roll over in her grave, but she was dead and since none of the boo-hoo brothers would make it through a eulogy, we blubbered approval. Please picture this next scene: St Luke's Episcopal Church in Anchorage where three generations have religiously attended beneath the stained-glass window donated by Dad. Mom's casket makes its way down the aisle with four grandsons on each side and three granddaughters following, passing by the four brothers in the Tyler front row. As many who attended stated afterward, "That's one close family!" Coogie and Two had done it all! I was surprised the sanctuary wasn't flooded by the tears coming from just the front row. Suddenly my slow critical thinking brain kicked into gear and I realized once again that life is fragile and it can end at any time, so after 20 years of a-pack-a day Marlboro habit, I quit. I guess because I had too much education, I was executor for both Mom and Dad. Before the year was out, I had convinced the other brothers that we ought to contribute a small amount of inheritance to establish an investment fund, the proceeds from which could only be used each year for the four of us to get together. We decided Dad would be proud if we did and the Tyler Reunion Trust (TRT) was founded and I managed the funds. Probably the best critical thinking decision we ever made and it is the glue that binds the family still.

The years 1995 and 1996 turned out to be the most tragic years yet for the Tyler Family. In August 1995, Gwathmey's wife Nina was diagnosed with late stage lung cancer. They moved son Gwathmey's wedding to Heather Kleisner up to November in Pittsburgh, Pennsylvania and Nina died less than three weeks later. It was right about this time that Beth was diagnosed with breast cancer and had a small lump removed. In June 1996 Terry's eldest son, Welby, died of a rare spleen disorder, for which he had been receiving treatments for about eight years. He was a soccer star, junior at Dad's alma mater, Duke University, and already, as a junior, had earned enough credits for a diploma. He was in Denver preparing to lead an Outward Bound camping week, when his body suddenly shut down. Terry was notified at 2 a.m. but could not get to him before he died. It stunned all of us. How could this happen? Terry probably summed it up best when he said the death of a child is just as horrible as the birth of a child is wonderful. We had hardly begun to grieve when we heard that Gwathmey's wife Nina had late stage lung cancer and was not expected to live long. They moved son Gwathmey's wedding to Heather Kleisner up to November in Pittsburgh, Pennsylvania, and Nina died less than three weeks later. It was right about this time that Beth was diagnosed with breast cancer and had a small lump removed. Not long thereafter she was diagnosed with Lupus, a tiring and debilitating disease that required strong medications over an extended period of time. Thankfully she was able to get on top of it after about 18 months and has been able to manage it successfully, thanks to a great doctor, good medication, diligence and patience on her part.

We didn't let much grass grow under TRT before writing checks. Our first stop (1993) was Figure 8 Island in South Carolina. We brought all the food, beer, liquor and wine for a week (took us a while to figure out you can go to a nearby grocery even at a beach resort) and divided up what nights each family would cook and clean up dinner. The week was a big success. So, we did it again the next year. On Friday morning, answering a knock at the door, we were greeted by a policeman, "May I please speak with a Mr. Tyler?" he inquired. The four brothers pointed at each other. "What seems to be the problem, officer?" we asked. It turns out two of Terry's sons, Welby and Lee, had incorrectly borrowed a Ski-do. Not invited back, the next year we moved south to Wrightsville Beach. After tragically losing Nina in late 1995, we needed something special in 1996. The Summer Olympics in Atlanta was the answer. Unable to get tickets for all of us to attend the same the event, we divided and conquered, with someone able to attend all the major events, including the opening, with surprise guest of Muhammed Ali, and closing ceremonies. The 1996 Atlanta Olympics were a big success for the city and all the Tylers.

With Charlie's Olympic efforts finished and the games complete, we took stock of TYFG and candidly found it lacking. We had done some great business and finally got paid on Capital City Plaza, but we had not added enough life insurance company type lenders to our stable, what's more, and after three years of Bill Clinton, the national economy was winding down and Atlanta's as well. Looking ahead, the deals were just not there. Even though our equity partner was willing to hang on, Charlie and I, thinking critically, decided to quit while we were ahead (barely), and shut it down. We gave the staff a month's pay and wished them well (they all found jobs relatively quickly). I set up shop in my basement (at Suite 1000, 3460 Paces Forest Dr. Atlanta, Georgia—who could tell?) with our number one assistant joining me two days a week to help get deals to potential lenders. Charlie took a great job at Price Waterhouse with a friend he first met at The Masters. Personally, I made as much money at home as I had at TYFG (just not the overhead).

HOLLIDAY FENOGLIO AND TYLER

When Bill Clinton *left* the White House, I left mine. I had seen this movie before. After eight years of ruinous left policies, I KNEW things would get much better under George W. Bush. Time to move to a much bigger platform. Holliday Fenoglio, in Houston, felt the same way. We were a perfect match of critical thinking gone right. John Fenoglio was everybody's favorite fraternity brother, and Hal Holliday was a classic Marine with Vietnam experience. Charlie and I actually courted them before we broke up and they declined, explaining they would have to invest their own money, which like us, was too dear at the time. They suggested Holliday Fenoglio and Tyler to get the local name recognition. Flattered, I agreed, leased office space in Buckhead and started hiring.

They had been in Houston for years, controlled most of the lenders and were the big gorilla. In Atlanta, at this point, Shoptaw James was the big gorilla, and would likely remain there. The main advantage I had was the ability to produce a structured finance product. You could charge more for it, but it took longer to produce and success was riskier. Most producers, given the lenders, would choose the conventional, simpler route. I didn't really have the choice. Holliday Fenoglio believed they could bring their lender relationships from Houston to Atlanta. Unfortunately, in those days, most lender relationships were geographically exclusive, meaning a lender dealt exclusively with Holliday Fenoglio in Houston, and only with Shoptaw James in Atlanta. A few would break ranks, but not many. At the end of the first year, Holliday and Fenoglio were not happy with my level of production and because they had taken in a bigger partner with more local relationships in Boston with John Fowler, they changed the name to Holliday Fenoglio and Fowler. I agreed, but really had no choice. Since over the phone, Fowler sounds so much like Tyler, you could hardly tell the difference. Keep moving. The numbers were not much better the next year. They weren't happy because they were not making much money, and neither was I for the same reason. They refused to admit that the Atlanta operation would never be the same as the Houston operation. It must be Tyler's fault. No changes yet, but I didn't like the smell of things. Sometimes critical thinking just stinks! The next year they decided to try a change—bring in their own man. By their own admission, they didn't like this guy when he first came with them and neither did their lenders. They then systematically broke him down mentally until he broke out crying in a meeting, and then rebuilt him in their own image! And now he was ready to come to Atlanta to help manage the office. With this by way of introduction, I really didn't think I was going to like this guy, but, I not only didn't like the guy, I totally despised him!

And he brought an assistant with him, who was just as obnoxious. No one in my office liked either one of them. They began to look elsewhere and so did I. Soon enough, Dennis James gave me a call and offered to buy my lunch. Dennis and I had known each other for years as friendly competitors. He said he wanted to hire me and I asked him why. He added that he needed someone in his shop to do structured finance deals. He further explained that his guys really didn't know how to do them and were spoiled doing easy life company deals. After chewing it over for a couple of weeks, I said let's cut a deal and that under no circumstances did I want to manage anything. He agreed, gave me plenty of salary, generous commission, and added that I could hire, train and fire, if needed, my own analyst. I moved into their offices and for the first time in decades I was working for someone else and free to do whatever I wanted. It felt great!

BACK TO THE NEW AND IMPROVED CBRE

About six months passed. Dennis called me into his office and asked what I knew about CBRE and Brian Stoffers. I told him, as he knew, it had been about 20 years since I left, but from what I knew they had grown a lot on the sales, management and leasing side, but I wasn't sure where they were on the finance side. I added that Brian Stoffers was a great guy who had run the San Diego Office when I had run Atlanta. He said that CBRE had made him an offer for his company and that Brian was coming to Atlanta to finalize the deal and talk to the entire office about any questions we may have. I called Brian right away and asked him what exactly he was doing. He said that he had been promoted to run both finance and brokerage and his charge was to grow finance and that was why he was coming to town. I congratulated him and caught him up on where I had been and how I got with Dennis. He asked if Dennis was a great as he seemed and about the rest of the team. I responded that the rest of the team were life company guys with a long history, that Dennis was the real thing and I was looking forward to his visit. Talk about a 180 degree turn around! The CBRE I had left was run by a brokerage; the one I was about to join was being run by a finance guy, and Jim Didion having lost the battle, was retiring. This was the answer to my old question about who should own a real estate finance company—real estate finance should own the whole company! It was great to see Brian again, and he made a great presentation. When the team asked what changes he would be making, he responded that when they buy a company, they buy it to make money and not to make changes. He added, "Just keep doing exactly what you are doing." In closing, he explained that we might want physically to move in with the brokerage division like most of the other finance divisions, but that could be our decision. What more could I possibly want? Home at last!

When we last visited my family, the Dynasty was 16 large and Meg and Will were in the Pace Academy lower school. I joined the Board of Trustees thanks to Neely Young, the assistant Headmaster. I quickly learned four important things:

I was the poorest member of the Board; our main job was to hire and fire Headmasters as needed; give and raise a lot of money; and finally I had a lot more to learn. Our current Headmaster had been there about 20 years, was an ex-Marine and loved by most but not all. Being a Headmaster is the hardest job in the world because of all the masters he must answer to—Board of Trustees, Parents, Alumni, teachers and students. Schools need Marines in the beginning to hire teachers for no salaries, find property, raise money daily, recruit students, teach, etc. Eventually it all gets too big and you have to delegate responsibility. Marines do not delegate well. So, we fired the Marine and searched for an experienced manager. Hired one, wrong one. Hired another. Finally fired the third, hired the fourth, and I stepped down from active Board duty. Critical thinking thing learned—most Headmasters should leave after six to eight years. They usually make more promises than they can keep and can no longer be effective.

At about this time Meg's career at Pace began to take off with her strong musical gifts for the school. She was Gretel in The Pace Academy production of the musical, "The Sound of Music" when she was in the second grade. Her senior year she was Sarah Brown in the musical "Guys and Dolls". Having good grades, good testing, stage experience in lead roles, voice lessons and quality recommendations, she applied to the top musical programs at the major Universities. She went to Northwestern University's summer musical training program the summer of her junior year, made the wait list there, and was offered a partial scholarship at a quality program in nearby Furman University. The net cost of attending Furman was half of Northwestern's cost which was $32,000 before annual increases. After strong urgings from Gwathmey (but no contribution), weighing the quality of the programs and considering the strong desires of the applicant, we chose Northwestern and were glad we did. After plenty of hard college work, numerous recitals, concerts and serving as president of her sorority, Meg was offered and accepted a job directing the middle school chorus at The Wesleyan School in suburban Atlanta following graduation. She grew her first-year chorus of 35 students to 125 her second year at Wesleyan and went on to be the director of the school music program and currently is director of all fine arts after 15 years.

MEG MARRIES JEFF FOSTER

A*round 18 months after* starting at Wesleyan, Meg called and asked me to take her beau Jeff, who directed the marching band and ran the upper school music program at Wesleyan, to play golf. I responded that music people don't play golf. She argued that this one does. We met at my house and drove to Ansley Golf Club. He was beating me like a drum when we stepped into the tee box on number 18, a par three, when we watched his tee shot bounce once on the green, then roll into the cup. It was the first hole in one I had ever seen. This was his second ace. Into the clubhouse to buy everyone there a drink, then off to my house, where he asked if Beth and I could spare a minute. He then asked permission to marry Meg. Hell, we had just met the guy, but if Meg liked him, he seemed qualified to us. Next came a big tented, catered, engagement party at our house and the now famous Music Man toast written by me, given by the four brothers, and appearing in the appendix. The following June, they were married at a church next to our house and the reception was held at Ansley Golf Club with a lot of Tyler chicanery, traditions and a late night "miss-step." The wedding was a thing of beauty from the flowers to the string quartet, to the participants. Beth and I walked down the aisle a little too early which made for a long wait for me standing there waiting for the arrangement to end. After some critical thinking I decided to ease the tension by whispering to Jeff, "Thanks for coming"—he doubled over. Will had agreed to sing a love song picked by Meg and arranged by Jeff. He strapped on his guitar and joined by the string quartet, sang a love ballad that brought the house to tears. Meg, the actress that she is, arm and arm with Jeff, marched out of that ceremony to conquer the world, to the applause and cheers by all those who attended. Starting with the chicanery, following the wedding, my job was to take some flowers by the house and then meet Beth and the rest of the guests at Ansley. Driving up to the house, I recognized all the brothers' cars and was greeted by the SOBs, drinks in hand, food on the table, in my den, watching my TV. They couldn't wait long enough to go to Ansley to watch the Belmont! I told them to get the hell out of my house, they had plenty of TVs, food, drinks, bands, and reception for them at the club, and slammed the door behind me. Strong memo to follow! At Ansley, the wedding party photos were just being finished and guests were arriving. The Tyler wedding tradition is for the Bride and Groom to cut the cake with the Tyler sword presented by the couple married previously. I made an announcement for all the guests who could hear me to go out on the porch and look toward the 18th tee. There, a bagpiper led the last couple, Courtney and Shay, from the tee, over the bridge, onto the green where Shay grabbed the flag from the hole and waved it all the way into the clubhouse to the cake cutting already in progress. My guess is maybe half the guests saw the ceremony, the rest eating, drinking, and gabbing amongst themselves (led by the brothers). In short order the band began to play, the ceremonial dances were danced, more drinks were poured and things got louder and faster. Then one of Meg's male friends decided that he needed to dance with the five-year old ring bearer, Jeff's nephew, whereupon he lost his balance, dropped Mitchell and broke his arm. I arrived upon the scene about the time Mitchell's mother was diagnosing the arm as being broken and requesting an immediate escort to the hospital. I was appointed the designated driver, suddenly sobered up, summoned my car, and carefully drove to the hospital. By the time we got back, Meg tossed the bouquet, gave me a kiss, and left with Jeff in the limo. Beth and I arrived home to a wrecked house and empty bar. After roasting the brothers, I scraped together the dregs of several bottles, and Beth, completely out of her beloved white wine, held her nose for one more drink and we fell into bed. After spending what amounted to three years of Northwestern tuition for a grand and memorable affair, we were not happy. C'est la vie. Audrey Elizabeth Foster was born August 18, 2008 and Eva Joyce joined them March 31, 2011. The Tyler Dynasty had grown to 21.

  Will closely followed his sister's act and some think he did her one better. As a young boy, he played Buckhead baseball and developed a beautiful, but often unproductive, swing. At Camp Dudley he picked up lacrosse which few in Atlanta played and wisely changed sports in his junior year. He said the main reason he favored lacrosse was because parents weren't the experts at it. In the process, he achieved the Rank of Eagle Scout which few of his classmates or even his father achieved. A proud moment for us both. On the Pace Stage, he also started young as one of the lost boys in "Peter Pan". As a junior, he starred as Curley in "Oklahoma" with a memorable opening, descending the stairs through the audience toward the stage in his cow boy boots and hat singing "Oh what a beautiful morning, Oh what a beautiful day." His senior year he played an even more challenging role as the lead in "Kiss Me Kate." His melodious baritone voice was improving daily.

We went on the college tour to Washington and Lee, Rhodes College and a few others we thought could be a good fit. Will's grades had been improving but were not stellar and his SAT scores were about average, but likely better than mine. We agreed it would be best to highlight his singing and acting talents. Before I knew it, he had applied early acceptance to Rhodes College and was accepted. I told him he should not have done that because he might have been able to win a talent scholarship of some sort. He disagreed, but I called them to double check. They responded that three years prior they had changed their admission practice and started awarding scholarships to the most qualified applicant who had auditioned, regardless of whether or not they had already committed to attending Rhodes. Long story short, he was awarded a half full scholarship for singing, and we found out later that the drama department was willing to offer him one also. Will pledged Phi Kappa Alpha and in his sophomore year was elected Mr. Rhodes.

After graduation in 2003, before I knew it, Will joined my company, CBRE as a property manager, his mother's profession, and his first big break came within six months. A large commercial real estate landlord in downtown Memphis hired the current CBRE manager that had the account for an in-house assignment, and asked CBRE to provide a replacement. They had rejected all five candidates CBRE had offered when Will got his shot. He sold them on the fact that their requirement was a 24-hour job and he had nothing else to do, was single, lived five minutes away, and had all the resources of big CBRE to draw on. He won the position AND the CBRE Rookie of the Year Award, something I have never seen since with any company, anywhere. To add insult to injury, his full-page picture appeared on the front page of "The Memphis Business Chronicle" while my largest photo ever was a one inch by one inch. Proud but painful! Four years later, when he decided to come home because his sister was having children and his mother had a heart operation, it was the wife of the Pace Theater director whom Beth had introduced to property management years earlier who offered him a job at Collier's Property Management. When Will first got into the business, I told him if he ever wanted to make money, he would need to leave property management and get into the commission-based transaction side of the business. About 18 months after joining Colliers, Will called and, asking if I had remembered my advice to him, proudly stated he had taken the first step toward the transition, "I HATE property management!" Within sixty days he was an office leasing agent at Collier's International.

    I will say one thing about Will. When it comes to women, he is very particular, very patient, and only goes first class. In high school, somehow, he decided to cut blonds out completely. In Memphis he began working with Episcopal youth groups, usually playing guitar and leading the singing. Two or three times when he came home, he brought two or three co-workers with him for lunch at our house. They were all attractive, but one, in particular, stood out from the crowd in my mind. As they were leaving one time, I caught Will's attention and pointed to my favorite. He later acknowledged my revelation, but added that she was dating someone else. He waited confidently and patiently. Her name was Hayley Arehart from Memphis and a graduate of The University of Tennessee. She was a youth group volunteer for her local Episcopal church and that is how they met. She clearly met all of Will's rigorous standards. Very attractive, bright and talented.

WILL AND HAYLEY GET MARRIED

Two years later, *The Tyler Clan assembled* in Kanuga, North Carolina, at another TRT sponsored event, this time at The Episcopal Church Retreat for Will's marriage to Hayley Jean Arehart. She had received permission from the Episcopal Bishop to hold their wedding ceremony at Kanuga. The property features a small hotel with dining facility, about a dozen cabins within easy walking distance, an event pavilion for the reception, a beautiful chapel for the wedding and a scenic lake. Hayley and Will did a great job explaining the set-up and accommodations to all the guests and made the reservations accordingly. Interestingly, many people were nervous about how rustic it might be and chose the hotel option or made a separate reservation at a motel in town. Most guests who had motel accommodations canceled them after they saw what was in store. Beth and tireless neighbor Connie Muldoon, bought, arranged and placed all the flowers which were plentiful and beautiful.

Will and all the groomsmen decorated the pavilion for the reception. The ceremony itself was a beautiful family affair—Audrey, five, and Eva, two, tossed rose petals as they danced down the aisle, and Meg sang "Ave Maria" accompanied by a piano and Jeff on the trumpet. The only Tyler mishap was brother Gwathmey who jumped into the lake with his hearing aid on. Another grand wedding and successful TRT event.

Will, being the real estate wizard that he is, found an ancient starter home just four miles south of our home in Smyrna. It was built in the 1920s, with three bedrooms, two baths at the end of a dead-end street, with plenty of room for their three dogs (Hayley is currently seeking treatment for her rescue dog addiction). The home was an easy commute to Will's office and easier commute to Hayley's job as the art teacher at the St. Benedict School which included grades from Kindergarten through eighth grade only one mile south of our house.

It was three years later that Henry Colgan Tyler arrived March 15, 2017. From 2004-2017 a wedding or birth occurred about every six months on average. The Tyler Dynasty is now 32 with one more already promised for 2018.

LIFE'S UNEXPECTED PLEASURES

You never know where life will lead you, especially if it involves your children. Clearly the biggest unexpected pleasure in our lives has been musical theater. Pace Academy already had a powerful musical theater tradition when we arrived and we found out how powerful when Meg was in the second grade and was cast as the youngest Van Trapp, Gretel, in the" Sound of Music". Since Pace had no stage of its own, they were forced to rent one off site which left very little time for rehearsals on their actual performance stage. That all ended my first year as a trustee when construction started, on a state of the art, 650-seat Fine Arts Center with all the bells and whistles including a deep performance stage; orchestra pit; attached set production facility with storage; advanced technical facilities including lighting, sound, and silent HVAC systems beneath the seats. Beth is a seamstress and immediately got into making costumes, which she still does on a $5,000 sewing machine. I, as a trustee, raised money for the facility, primarily from the parents. By design we wanted our children to know we were investing our money, time and talent into their efforts and talent. We became good friends with George Mengert, the director and his wife Annette, with whom Beth got started in the real estate property management business. We were deeply involved in about 15 Pace Musicals, and as an adjunct, went to New York and London for about 10 more professional productions and even got to see our children perform at Carnegie Hall. Who would ever have guessed we would be involved in 25 Musicals? It was a blast. As a by-product of serving as a Trustee, I developed lasting friendships with some of the most talented, successful and generous people I have ever known. Chuck Brady, former President of Life of Georgia, and his wife Betsy were at the top of the list. He, without a doubt, was the best salesman I ever knew (maybe except for my father). Randolph Goulding, owner of a private engineering firm and his wife Charlotte, eventually were our neighbors where we currently live, were living models on how to have meaningful lives as senior citizens into retirement. Mark Dunaway, who never finished college, and his wife, Marsha were the epitome of generosity, and an inspiration to me in running my own company. Eddie Mendel, who managed the fortunes of the wealthiest families in Atlanta and his wife Barbara, taught me all I needed to know about managing my own money. And finally, John and Anne Parker, who are among the wealthiest families at Pace are quietly the most generous with their wealth, their time, their home and their talent. He owns his law firm, is an active Republican fundraiser and a Duke graduate while she, a proud and loud UVA graduate is an extremely talented interior designer and Bible study leader and organizer. Our Meg and their daughter, Blair, are best friends so we got to know them very well. The Third Musketeer was also a Pace student, Amanda Hoffman. A mother/daughter senior year Easter Weekend extravaganza, planned and executed by Anne, included Blair, Amanda, Meg, Ree, Amanda's mom, and Beth and featured a limo in Atlanta to the airport, flight to New York City, limo to the Waldorf Hotel (which included a spacious suite at economy pricing because the Hotel messed up and Anne negotiated a stellar deal), dinner at a signature restaurant followed by Julie Andrews in the Broadway show, "Victor, Victoria". Saturday all day shopping at posh stores with professional cab hailing by Anne, more fine dining, and thanks to Anne's expertise at the ticket broker window that afternoon, "How to Succeed in Business" on Broadway that evening, Sunday started with Easter Mass at Trinity Cathedral followed by a limo to the airport, flight to Atlanta and limo home for weary travelers welcomed by broke fathers. The Parkers hosted a wedding brunch for the brothers and others at their oft used, beautiful home for Meg and Jeff's wedding. Anne picked out all the colors for walls and ceilings in our current and final home (I never knew the color of the ceiling could completely change a painting in a room), and the list goes on and on. Their only flaw is they never let us reciprocate.

Now Pace was not the only place we enjoyed friends. In the early days in Morningside, Shelly and Rusty McDougal were our new best friends with their two sons, Scott and John matching those of Meg and Will, and he became our dentist. The moms would meet regularly in Noble Park which was between our houses. Hoby and Anne Warner, our friends from Emory Business School with daughters Dru (my Goddaughter) and Catherine who were older than ours, were regulars as well. The Warner Family, and Joan and Mike Walters plus their two daughters Caroline and Meredith, who matched well with the Warner girls, joined the Tyler family each spring for a long weekend at FDR State Park, about an hour away. We would haul all our provisions to three cabins in the park, act like we were fishing in the nearby pond (never caught one fish), and the kids learned about frogs and tadpoles. Mike and Joan and Beth were friends from a previous life; he was a UVA grad as was Hoby, and he was director of Human Resources at Coca-Cola. Hoby, Mike and I usually left early enough to play a round of golf on Friday, and the wives and kids would join us in time for cocktails. After putting the children down, we would gather in one cabin, commence drinking, discussing the economy and politics mostly. Anne, the leading liberal in the group, certainly spiced things up, but always held her own. On more than one occasion, things got pretty heated and had to be broken up by an adult in the room who had not yet taken a side in the ruckus (not me). Late one particular night, Mike said he had an announcement to make but we could never breathe a word of it until we had read or heard about it otherwise, likely Monday morning. On Monday Coke would announce, that they, in addition to "old" Coke, would be selling "new" Coke which, after extensive taste studies, they had recently developed. Mike said that he and the Company believed without a doubt, this would revolutionize Coke and the beverage industry and Coke's stock would go through the roof. Hoby, a stock analyst, vehemently disagreed. His reasoning primarily was that Coke had spent years and billions of dollars telling the world that "old" Coke was the best tasting beverage in the world, and the world would now think they had been lied to. The rest of us didn't know what to think, but it was certainly interesting to contemplate this upcoming global event in the solitude of FDR State Park! It probably took the better part of a year to prove, but Hoby was right. Always mindful of playmate balance, several winters we made a trip to Beech Mountain, North Carolina, with Amanda and Andrew Hoffman, perfect age match with Meg and Will and mom Ree. Skiing was not my sport as you may have guessed, but I tried to at least be helpful to the others who really enjoyed it. On one of the trips, we received a surprise phone call from our housekeeper in Atlanta, who had discovered that our house had been robbed by the perpetrators throwing a bird bath through a rear window. The housekeeper was a little shaken, but had called the police and stayed with them as they toured the damage. She continued that they had ransacked our bedroom and a playroom in the basement. We told her it was best not to touch or bother cleaning anything and to take pictures if she could and make sure she locked up. When we inspected the wreck and inventoried what we thought was missing, we determined the burglers had gotten only some costume jewelry from Beth's dresser and my grandfather's 100 year-old gold pocket watch. As for the playroom mess, it appeared the perpetrators there were only Meg and Will. After going to about every pawn shop I could think of in ninety days, and checking back with the police for an update, I was just about ready to give up when Beth showed up dangling the watch by its chain. It turns out that thanks to critical thinking, we had cleverly hidden the watch in Will's sock drawer and forgotten it. Andrew Hoffman, Phillip Cramner, and Will, often the Three Musketeers around Pace, three years later were given their Eagle Scout awards together. In summary, the more time, effort and money you put into your children their friends, and parents, the more everyone gets out of it.

Not everything was centered around our children, though. Tom and Julia Wratten of Naples are very good mortgage friends with whom we spent a lot of time at the Mortgage Bankers' Convention. Stan and Barbara Ackeman, a mortgage lender who lived in New York City and were a huge part of our visits with them in the City at some great restaurants. Charlie O'Donnell ran the Hackensack, New Jersey office for CBRE, when I ran Atlanta. He made plenty of trips to Atlanta, introduced me to numerous New York lenders and Beth and I loved going to New York and painting the town red with Charlie and wife Pat. Old friends, Dr. Gil Burke, wife Carol, and three daughters Emily, Julie, and Katherine used to vacation at Myrtle Beach in September before the children had to be in school at that time. We would rent a house and they would bring their maid, Bessie. We also spent many a party night at their cabin on the Blue Ridge Parkway. Unfortunately, Dr. Gil died on my birthday in 2002, for which I will never forgive him, but we try to see Carol and at least some of the girls once a year. Dr. Bob Steele and his wife Julie were on the party list whenever we got together with the Burkes and afterwards at Bob and Julie's condo at Kiawah Island, South Carolina, around New Years. Unfortunately, Julie passed away in 2016 from ovarian cancer.

Then there were the random trips to Chicago and Evanston when Meg was at Northwestern, to Memphis when Will attended Rhodes and to New York City to see both Meg and Will sing at famous Carnegie Hall and take in few Broadway shows. Somehow, we never got around to doing the USA tour with the children, but I think we made up for it on a three- week driving tour of England and Scotland, with Will videoing our "we're lost again" arguments from the backseat. For our 20th wedding anniversary we cruised around the entire boot of Italy for two weeks, somehow missing Bo and Margaret's wedding, and we celebrated our 40th with Johnny and Gretchen Clark and two other Louisville couples on a two- week riverboat cruise from Prague to Budapest. To give you a clue how things change, on the first cruise, Beth insisted that we not know anyone else on the cruise so we could be alone, and on the second, she welcomed the three other couples calling it insurance in case something happened to me. The "Lifetime Achievement Awards" go to Weezie and John Magnusson for Weezie being Godmother to Gwathmey Tyler IV, born June 5, 1969, the first Tyler grandchild and cousin number five and William Colgan Tyler, Jr. born March 30, 1983, the last of the grandchildren and cousin number 16, and also Beth's Uncle Joe Hardin, who during his lifetime attended every event that Meg and Will participated in from swim meets, to baseball games, to Pace musicals.

And finally, the "Glue Award" goes to TRT for nine regular beach weeks, six weeks at Terry's and Robin's house at Debordieu, three mountain trips and the special event trips including: The 1996 Summer Olympics in Atlanta, The Colgan Reunion, Durango Colorado, Maitland Reunion, Kirkudbright, Scotland, Little Diamond Island, Portland, Maine, and Capon Springs, West Virginia, for a total of 23 straight Tyler Reunions! Join the Tyler Clan and see the world! One quick shout out to the most dependable emotion of them all- greed-my favorite. The four Brothers all practiced greed after we invested our small inheritance into TRT and attended every reunion so no other Brother would get our share. So eventually when we had so many cousins, we expanded the opportunity to practice greed by requiring each adult cousin to invest $100 every year to grow the corpus. Voila—perfect TRT attendance every year. Works every time.

I sincerely hope you have learned something about the benefits of critical thinking by taking this long journey with the Tyler family. In closing, please pardon my blatant plagiarizing as I say farewell from the Tyler Clan, where the women are strong, all the men are good looking and the children are above average.

And that's the way it is, Thursday, November 10, 2017. Good night and good luck.

Will and Hayley get married

Tyler family in Bill Tyler's backyard

Bill and Beth at Jeff and Meg's wedding

Judy and Gwathmey circa 2014

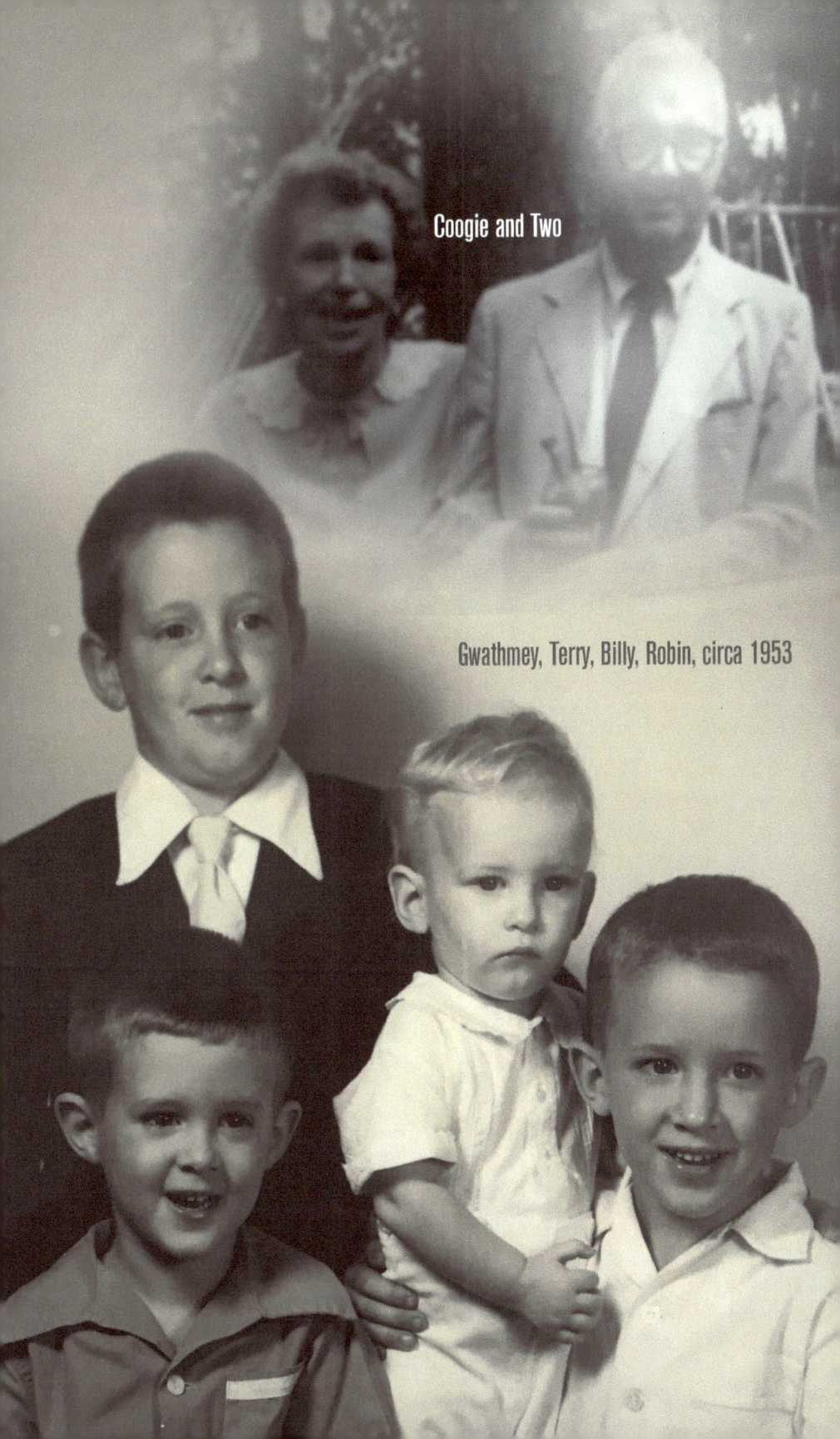

Coogie and Two

Gwathmey, Terry, Billy, Robin, circa 1953

Claudia & Sam Bonefishing in Bahmas

Welby

Tyler clan at Big Canoe

...elby, Terry, Courtney, Mandy, and Lee

...ndy, Logan, Eloise, Courtney, and Baylor

Eloise

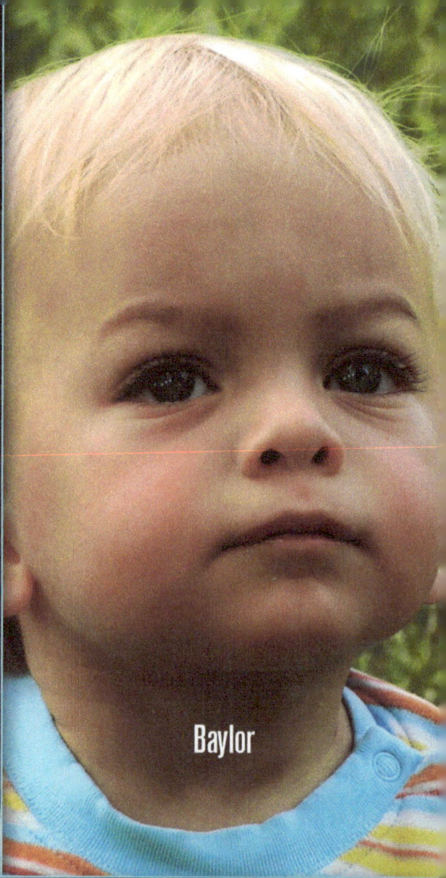

Baylor

Logan

Lee, Courtney, and Welby

Gwathmey and Judy on wedding night

Terry, Gwathmey, Robin, and Billy

Hayley & Will Tyler's Wedding

The Foster Family

www.ingramcontent.com/pod-product-compliance
Lightning Source LLC
Chambersburg PA
CBHW041618220426
43661CB00030B/1327/J